Alcohol-Free ENTERTAINING

Alcohol-Free ENTERTAINING

Come for Mocktails

◆

Patsy Bickerstaff
Bill Seay

Betterway Publications
White Hall, Virginia

Published by Betterway Publications, Inc.
White Hall, VA 22987

Cover design by Julienne McNeer

Library of Congress Cataloging-in-Publication Data
Bickerstaff, Patsy Anne,
    Alcohol-free entertaining.

    Includes index.
    1. Beverages. 2. Entertaining. I. Seay, Wilson
    Lee   II. Title.
TX815.B49   1985   641.2′6   85-46057
ISBN 0-932620-59-0 (pbk.)

Printed in the United States of America
0 9 8 7 6 5 4 3 2 1

Dedication

◆

To doctors and pilots who must stay alert,
   To folks who play tennis and run;
To smart volunteers who are driving back home
   After the party is done;
To people whose livers are still good as new,
   To those who have battled and won.

Lift up your Mocktails in praise of yourself;
   Here's to your health . . . and have fun!

Table of Contents

Introduction

◆

To Your Health!
With a Mocktail!

Time was, when a card came in the mail, saying, "Everybody said I had a wonderful time!" it meant you were the perfect host, or hostess. You may have had to send your floors out to be laundered, hire an archaeologist to retrieve the hors d'oeuvres out of the furniture, and redecorate the living room in guacamole green, but your party was a success.

Rules for gracious entertaining dictated that you *must* be able to serve everybody's favorite "poison," (a surprisingly accurate term) be it Royal or Ripple; you *must* urge everyone to "have just one more" when you meant "Go home, Lush!" and you *must* have a bartender who could pour a perfect pousse-cafe, and mix a Dragon's Breath or even a Rotten Robert without hesitating.

After following the rules for years, you may have noticed that the only people who really enjoyed parties were little kids at birthday bashes, and the non-drinkers telling jokes over the snack table. But the parties didn't change much.

Along came what is fondly known as "the health kick." Men began running around the block in their underwear, with or without the neighborhood dogs. Women discovered "aerobics," a form of voluntary physical torture performed in expensive leotards and accompanied by bad music. This was great for the muscles. Smokers, with a little encouragement and a lot of nagging, discarded their cigarettes. This was great for the lungs. Chubby people began to slim down, substituting vitamins for bonbons. This was great for the heart. Superman and Wonder Woman were multiplied by the hundreds.

It was inevitable that somebody would recognize that muscles and lungs and hearts aren't worth a darn without livers and stomachs. Besides, there was a distinctly unhealthful propensity toward motor vehicle collisions on the part of those people with 80-proof breath and fried eyeballs. With the cost of automobiles going up, and the traffic authorities cracking down, other health considerations became evident. There's not much time to exercise when you have to work three jobs to pay car insurance premiums, and broken bones inhibit the development of good muscle tone. And the jails don't serve gourmet health foods. This meant crisis time for the party people.

First Lady Rosalynn Carter made a brave start by eliminating the booze at White House parties. The move wasn't popular, especially with her brother-in-law, and it didn't catch on right away, but it didn't seem to hurt anyone. Grudgingly, and usually in private, there was recognition of the fact that lowering the octane was a good idea, but it didn't sound like fun. There had to be a solution.

One popular way out of the quandary is the Mocktail Party. Smart hosts and hostesses have begun entertaining with parties that include sparkly, original drinks featuring fruit juice, colas, hints of cooking extract, ice cream — anything but alcoholic beverages.

Is it possible to "unwind" without anesthesia? Watch the little kids, and the gang at the snack table. Yes, it's possible, but maybe some will have to learn how. Will they be willing to learn? They'd better be.

There are plenty of non-alcoholic beverages available. Fruit and vegetable juices, soft drinks, tea and coffee have been around all the time. In addition, new products like no-booze beer and sparking fruit juices are appearing on the scene.

Straight from the bottle or "a la rocks," pre-packaged refreshments can be served with ease. But for the additional fun of serving a variety of specialties with creativity and panache, this book is just the thing.

All the recipes have been carefully measured and tested, and are ready to use. If you want to experiment a little, and add a few of your own, good for you. The undeniable fact is that mocktail drinkers last longer, and as even Shakespeare could have told you, make better lovers. As you become part of the new generation of Mocktail Party hosts, enjoy yourself, your company, and good health.

Chapter One

What's a Mocktail
and
Who Wants One?

Chapter One
◆

The word "mocktail" seems to have originated in the Eastern United States, possibly in Washington, D.C., about 1984. There's not really any documentation to prove that point, so if you know better, you know better. It means, quite simply, a "mock cocktail," a non-alcoholic beverage which replaces a traditional mixed drink. They've been around for a long time, but until recent years, they were considered to be something reserved for children. Adults were supposed to drink stronger stuff.

If you're a non-alcohol drinker, you'll know that last statement is no exaggeration. In high school, you were affectionately termed a "nerd" or whatever the expression was in your generation. Your college classmates, a little more sophisticated and tolerant, just considered you sort of strange. Later, your neighbors scratched your name from their party lists, because they thought you didn't like having fun, or assumed that you "must have a problem." Oddly enough, they kept inviting people who obviously *did* "have a problem," and tolerating the embarrassment. Meanwhile, waitresses giggled when you ordered a Shirley Temple in a restaurant, and all your friends kept urging you to "try this," or "have just one," because that was supposed to be polite.

If you do drink, and serve, alcoholic beverages, you've been under an equally unpleasant kind of pressure. If you were young, you were supposed to try to match the "good ol' boys" drink for drink without losing your balance, even if they were twenty years older and fifty pounds heavier. You "needed" to get drunk at least once, and a brawl or automobile collison made you a folk hero. Your parties cost a fortune, because you had to stock everybody's favorite. If someone turned down your whiskey, you were a poor host, and you were expected to urge your guests to overdo it, then spend the night. All this was supposed to be "civilized."

In the past several years, though, Americans have begun to take a different point of view. Health, fitness and safety have begun to take precedence over social customs that didn't make much sense, and were frequently harmful. People are reducing their consumption of alcohol, or cutting it off altogether, and the mocktail party is replacing Happy Hours with a sophisticated pleasure and, in many quarters, a sigh of relief. But it's happened so gradually, so subtly, that a lot of old-timers are left wondering, "How did we get here?"

That's a fair question, and the answer is interesting enough to explore. The movement that has been called "a new temperance" has several roots, most of which go back to good old common sense.

Certainly, one factor to be considered is the American obsession with being thin. People who are overweight are considered less attractive-looking, less intelligent, and less capable of self-control than their thinner neighbors. It isn't an accurate evaluation, but it leads millions of us to diet, exercise and generally watch our waistlines. And alcohol is full of calories! Not only that, they aren't even nutritious calories. As the desire to be thin has expanded to include the desire to be strong, healthy and active, alcohol has had a harder and harder time fitting into the lifestyle of the body-conscious American.

A related factor comes from the attention given by the Surgeon General, and a lot of other physicians, to the effect of certain substances on the human body. A heavy-handed anti-tobacco campaign has made poeple think twice about some of the other things they've been ingesting. If smoking was bad for them, many people reasoned, drinking booze must be as bad, or worse. As a result, they tried reducing or eliminating their intake. When they realized they felt better, that was enough evidence to make them change their habits.

The "horror stories" haven't escaped us, either. With 15 million Americans suffering from chemical dependency, we've seen friends, relatives, and favorite celebrities suffer from the damaging effects of alcoholism, from simply embarrassing themselves, to committing crimes, to death. Alcoholism is the third largest killer in the United States, and that doesn't even count the suicides, murders, and automobile fatalities. Nor does it count the alcohol-related cancer and heart-disease deaths. They're in another category.

As traffic fatalities mount, public safety officials everywhere look for ways to reduce the slaughter. The 55-mph speed limit helps. Seat belts help. But one-half of the fatal accidents are still caused by drinking drivers. Laws and organizations were set up to "get tough" with this kind of recklessness, and people are beginning to get the message. After all, a jail sentence can do wonders to ruin your career.

Two courageous former First Ladies deserve some of the credit. When Betty Ford proved to the world that a chemical dependency can be defeated, she convinced a lot of other famous people to stop hiding their illness and fight it. Anyone planning a posh social event with a lot of "big names" these days had better feature non-alcoholic drinks, if only for the VIP's who've decided to get smart, get help and get sober. Rosalynn Carter's insistence on alcohol-free White House functions is no longer the rule, but it showed everyone that a sophisticated social event can take place without liquor.

More people than ever *can't* drink alcohol. Not just recovering alcoholics, but a number of people with other illnesses know that their health, even their lives may depend on an alcohol-free lifestyle. Persons with diabetes, hypoglycemia, liver and kidney and heart problems, some of whom might not have survived several years ago, supplement the blessings of medical science with a cautious responsibility about what goes in their bodies. Charter pilots and physicians with a high emergency caseload, who have to have clear judgment and excellent coordination on a moment's notice, are better off if they stick to soft drinks. Obstetricians and neurologists can't show up with shaky hands.

This brings us to the final factor. Many Americans are seeing sobriety as an occupational issue. In 1977, John Molloy, in *The Woman's Dress For Success Book*, was warning women to pass up the martinis at lunchtime if they wanted to be taken seriously on the job. They not only got the message, but apparently passed it on to their male colleagues by example, because according to all published reports, lunchtime drinking is down and business is being conducted over tea in gracious surroundings such as the Ritz-Carlton in Boston and the Waldorf-Astoria in New York. Bright young men and women know that one way to lose out to the competition for excellent jobs and promotions is to get drunk and look foolish in the wrong place. And the bright old men and women in the vice-president's chairs are fully aware that if they embarrass the company, there are plenty of nominees to replace them. In an interdependent society such as ours, there isn't room for the kind of poor performance that come with a "buzz" or a hangover. Lives depend on the accuracy of the assembly line worker who builds a car, the cleanliness of the packing-plant employee. Products liability and malpractice litigation warn us that work must be done right. That's why the companies are spending money to rehabilitate people with chemical-dependency problems, and that's why individuals who are looking out for their own careers are looking for alternatives to an alcohol-based social system.

And they're finding them. Many people are going to the same cocktail lounges that have always been around, but now they're ordering soft drinks and soda water. Others are frequenting newer establishments that feature "fizzies" and "frosties" as house specialties, alongside the familiar martinis. In large metropolitan cities, "beverage boutiques" or mocktail lounges, such as High Sobriety in Dallas, are springing up. The ambience of the cocktail lounge isn't lost, but all the drinks are alcohol-free, including de-alcoholized wine and beer and unfermented cider, for those who want a special kind of taste.

Then there are people like you, who choose to try entertaining with a mocktail party. They're finding, sometimes to their surprise, that all the money they used to spend on liquor wasn't really the guarantee of a good party. With imagination, cordiality, and relaxation, good friends are getting together all over America, to enjoy the flavor and fun without the hang-over.

How long will the new trend last? There is no shortage of predictions. A few cynics, who either make their money on spirits or don't like the idea of giving up their multi-martinis or being left behind, consider it a passing fad, the product of neo-prohibitionist "crazies." Others, who have recognized an advantage to themselves, don't care how long everybody else sticks with soda water; they've made up their minds, and changed their habits, for good. There's no real way to tell whether the ethyl reduction is going to be bigger or smaller, temporary or permanent. But it doesn't really matter. For now, at least, you've joined a generation of healthy, active fun-lovers who want to get everything out of life, including the enjoyment of reality. It's all available, with the today kind of refreshment you'll be serving.

Chapter Two

---◆---

Things
to
Know

Chapter Two

◆

The experienced bartender will have sub-
stantial familiarity with measurements, bar tools and tech-
niques. The long-time host who owns a good bar handbook
already has detailed descriptions, instructions and explanations
at his fingertips. If you fit either of these categories, the infor-
mation in this chapter won't be new to you. If not, and you're a
newcomer to the whole idea of drink-mixing, you'll pick up
the necessary helpful hints to begin.

Mocktails and their ingredients aren't burdened with the
legendry and ceremony that surround stronger spirits, so there
aren't many absolute do's and don't's to learn about time, place
and garnish. Nonetheless, a few guidelines and how-to's are in
order.

USEFUL EQUIPMENT

GLASS PITCHER: — For drinks that should be stirred, rather than shaken, to preserve clarity.

COCKTAIL SHAKER: — The less experienced person may prefer the home-type shaker, with pouring spout, over the professional bartender's set of metal and glassmixers.

ELECTRIC BLENDER: — For foamy and frosty drinks

BAR SPOON: — Long handle

BOTTLE OPENER

PIERCING CAN OPENER

MEASURING GLASS: — A graduated measure, marked from 1 to 6 oz. is easier to use, but a 1-oz. measure will do.

MEASURING SPOONS

ICE SCOOP

PARING KNIFE

GARNISH SPEARS OR TOOTHPICKS

SWIZZLE STICKS, STIRRERS, STRAWS

As you develop your own sophisticated specialties, you may wish to add more tools to make the job easier, but those listed above will give you a good beginning.

BASIC MEASUREMENTS

Some bar measurements become very large, very esoteric, and not too useful. For the mocktail maker's purposes, the following are sufficient.

Dash	⅛ teaspoon
Teaspoon (tsp.)	⅙ ounce
Tablespoon (Tbsp.)	½ ounce or 3 teaspoons
Cup	8 ounces or ½ pint
Pint	16 ounces
Quart	32 ounces

GLASSES AND WHAT TO DO WITH THEM

Part of your finished drink's image comes from the glass in which it is served. Traditional cocktails have been assigned to certain glasses, and in many cases, the glasses have become known by the names of their expected contents, such as champagne, martini, old-fashioned or high-ball. There are no hard-and-fast rules that apply to the glasses in which mocktails are served. This is partly because the mocktail trend is a fairly new one, and partly because alcohol-free drinks are so versatile. Orange juice, for example, may appear in a 6-ounce glass as part of breakfast, in a tall tumbler over ice after a brisk tennis game, or in a 4-ounce winestem as an appetizer at the evening meal. Tea and coffee may be served hot in small cups or large mugs, or iced in glasses. But the appeal of the mocktail, like that of its stronger cousins, is enhanced by a glass that "looks right.'' You'll notice that in this book, suggestions are given with each recipe. However, if something else "looks right" to you, or fits the mood of your particular festivity, it's equally correct.

If you want to become an expert on bar glassware, most bar handbooks can provide you with detailed descriptions, but for the recipes in this book, a few basic designs can be adaptable enough to serve any purpose.

For serving faux wines and some of the richer mocktails, you'll want 4-ounce stemmed wine or cocktail glasses. Because faux wines aren't subject to the customary swirling and sniffing, the glasses can properly be filled. The "one-third" full rule doesn't hold here. Stemmed champagne or sherbet glasses look elegant for faux champagne and some of the slushy-foamy dessert-type delicacies. Old-fashioned (6-8 ounce) and collins or high-ball (11-12 ounce) tumblers will complete your requirements, although you may wish to add, or substitute, stemmed water goblets.

CHILLING   Chill every glass before filling. This can be done by storing the glasses in the refrigerator for an hour, or in the freezer compartment for a few minutes. To chill in a hurry, fill glasses with crushed ice and stir.

FROSTING   Dip glasses in tepid water; while the glasses are still wet, store in freezer until frosty.

SUGAR FROSTING   Chill glasses, moisten rims with a wedge of lemon or lime, a piece of citrus peel, or syrup. Dip rims in superfine sugar.

READY-TO-SERVE TREATS

There's a world of delicious alcohol-free beverages available before you even start mixing. Supermarkets and gourmet food shops carry bottled sodas ranging from carbonated orange and cola to deli specialties like celery soda. Health-food stores, and the corner grocery, carry fruit and vegetable juices of all kinds, solo or blended into exotic concoctions. Any of these can be served with a flip of the opener, and many mix nicely in imaginative ways with other flavors.

WATER WISDOM

As a general rule, mocktails are less complicated than traditional alcoholic beverages, less shrouded in mystery and even snobbery. The one exception to that rule comes with the substance that is seemingly least complicated of all — water. We haven't yet reached the point of ordering water by the year, but the H_2O expert is beginning to rival the connoisseur of fine wines for status and sophistication. "Water snobs" are beginning to appear, each with his own opinion of one or more of the various bottled mineral waters.

To be fair, there's nothing new about a fascination with mineral water. Since ancient times, it has been credited with marvelous curative properties, and in America and abroad, elegant spas and resorts have been built around mineral springs. Examples are Warm Springs in Georgia, famous for the visits of Franklin Delano Roosevelt, and Saratoga in New York. Water from some of the many American springs is bottled for use nationwide, and takes its place alongside the European waters, both still and effervescent, and sparkling water from several companies, as one of the most popular potables of the day.

The following list covers some of the best-known varieties of mineral water and club sodas, with country of origin. No effort is made to describe or evaluate the tastes. You'll be able to follow the conversation of the water aficionados, but if you want to argue with them, you'll have to consult your most trusted expert, or do some taste comparisons of your own. There's a wide choice available, so you can pick your own favorite.

BOTTLED MINERAL WATER AND CLUB SODAS

Mountain Valley Mineral Water	USA (Hot Springs, Arkansas)
Vichy-Celestins	France
Vittel	France
Deer Park	USA (Maryland)
Evian	France
Appolinaris	West Germany
Poland Spring	USA (New Jersey)
San Pellegrino	Italy
Saratoga	USA (New York)
Carci-Crespo	Mexico
Perrier	France
Calistoga	USA (California)
Canada Dry	USA
White Rock	USA
Seagram's	USA
Schweppes	USA

All mineral water should be served chilled, and sometimes a trace of citrus flavor is added; the well-known Perrier, for example, has expanded its line to include lemon- and orange-flavored varieties, in addition to its familiar green bottle. The more expensive brands of mineral water may, if you like, be included in mocktail recipes requiring club soda. But when serving to "water freaks," it's a good idea to find out exactly how your guests want it. Some like a squeeze of lime; others prefer the taste "pure." Some like it "on the rocks" and some will tell you that ice bruises the bubbles. A remark like that can leave you wondering for a long time. One thing is certain; your guests won't be a bit shy about telling you the "best" way to enjoy their favorite.

STOCKING UP

If you already have a well-stocked bar, your supply of mixers, flavorings and garnishes puts you well on the way to being ready for a mocktail party. Add at least one "elite" effervescent mineral water, and you have the basis for a respectable repertoire of alcohol-free beverages. You will need to increase your estimate of drinks-per-person, though. One observation that has already been made is that mocktail parties last longer. Instead of "drifting," exchanging short greetings, guests are engaging in conversations, enjoying one another's company more than at the traditional cocktail party. Instead of the 2-3 drinks you've been serving, plan on 3 to 5 drinks per guest.

If you're new at party-giving, you'll need some guidelines for supplying yourself. First, read over the recipes for the drinks you expect to serve. Make sure you have all the necessary ingredients. If you're inviting a few friends over for a single kind of drink, such as strawberry mocquiris or piña con nadas, have a little cola or ginger ale handy for the individual who's allergic to strawberries or can't take coconut. When you plan to serve a variety of mocktails, be ready with a supply of "basics." The lists below will help.

CARBONATED BEVERAGES

COLA
GINGER ALE
LEMON LIME SODA (7-Up, Teem, Like, Sprite, Slice, etc.)
CLUB SODA or sparkling water for mixing
EFFERVESCENT MINERAL WATER to be served unmixed. (Perrier is a favorite in many places, and is a good standard, but another brand may be preferred in your neighborhood.)

You may want to add other familiar "mixers" such as Wink or Collins Mix, and don't forget good old coffee and tea, hot or iced, to fit the season.

JUICES

ORANGE   CRANBERRY
LEMON   TOMATO
GRAPEFRUIT

This list only scatches the surface. Apple, pineapple, and grape juices appear in many of these recipes, and others become a little more exotic, calling for papaya, raspberry, and others. Certainly, the array of juices is wide enough that your taste preference, imagination and pocketbook are the final guidelines to which one you'll want for your party.

FLAVORINGS

Because the drinks you're serving don't depend on alcoholic ingredients for taste, you'll want a variety of flavorings to give them their "personality." These flavorings will express your individuality and artistry. At least, you'll need:

SUPERFINE SUGAR   ANGOSTURA BITTERS
SIMPLE SYRUP   GRENADINE SYRUP
    (See Below)   ROSE'S LIME JUICE

In addition, you'll discover many syrups and extracts, some of which will substitute nicely for expensive liqueurs in "converted" drinks, such as Harvey's Brother, and others with their own inimitable quality for your more elaborate preparations. These include:

MARASCHINO SYRUP
CREME de MENTHE SYRUP
CREME de COCOA SAUCE
CREAM OF COCONUT
COOKING EXTRACTS: Rum, anise, mint, vanilla
PASSIONFRUIT SYRUP
CHOCOLATE SYRUP
MAPLE SYRUP
CONFECTIONER'S SUGAR
FRUIT, fresh, frozen or canned as required by recipe: Strawberries, raspberries, bananas, peaches.

SIMPLE SYRUP

You won't find simple syrup on your grocer's shelf. You make it at home, using this recipe:

1 cup sugar
1 cup water

Bring water to a boil Add sugar and simmer 1½ minutes. The liquid will be reduced to about 1 cup and have a light syrup consistency. Cool and bottle.

GARNISHES

Although garnishes are suggested throughout the book, there are very few mocktails for which a particular fillip is de rigueur. Of course, the Horse's Neck would only be a glass of ginger ale without its long strip of lemon peel, and the Shirley Temple usually sports a maraschino cherry, and occasionally an orange slice. But for the most part, the garnish that glamourizes your drink can be your own special touch. Some standards to have on hand are:

ORANGE SLICES   PINEAPPLE STICKS
LEMON WEDGES   CINNAMON
LIME WEDGES   NUTMEG
MARASCHINO CHERRIES

Other possibilities include bar foam or freshly beaten egg white, mixed bar fruits, mint sprigs and sometimes, small flowers.

FRESH CITRUS FRUITS AND PEELS

To get the most juice from citrus fruits, "tame" the fruit before cutting by rolling back and forth on a cutting board, leaning on the fruit with the palm of your hand. Cut slices thinner than ¼ inch, and cut orange slices in half. Quarter lemons and limes for wedges, and halve wedges again if too large. For recipes requiring fruit peel, cut off only the colored surface of the peel with a sharp paring knife or lemon stripper, just before serving to preserve the peel oils. When the peel of an entire lemon is necessary, peel carefully in a continuous unbroken spiral.

DRINK MIXES

Bottled or packaged mixes are available for a number of familiar cocktails. Any of these can be used, without the alcoholic ingredients, to mix the corresponding mocktail. If you feel more comfortable with a mix at first, use it, but in time, you'll take pride and pleasure in turning out, with confidence and expertise, your personal version of the nation's newest kind of refreshment — the Mocktail.

Chapter Three

·———◆———·

The
Wine
List

Chapter Three

As some partygoers have moved from stronger mixed drinks to wines, others have been moving from wine to even lighter beverages. Sparkling cider, dealcoholized wine and sparkling grape juices are available, elegantly bottled. In addition, you may choose to serve the following refreshing combinations of juices and ginger ale, every bit as delightful for celebrating, or for accompaniment to a special dinner, as the "originals."

SUPERSONIC SANGRIA

Ole´! A special party-maker using the new de-alcoholized wine.

For about 10 servings, combine in pitcher or punch bowl:

1 pint orange juice
8 ounces lemon juice
Superfine sugar or simple syrup to taste
1 bottle de-alcoholized red wine

Combine fruit juices with sugar or simple syrup and stir well (if sugar is used, stir until dissolved.) Chill and serve garnished with orange, lemon and lime slices.

FAUX CHAMPAGNE

Ring in the New Year with this festive beverage, and drive home after the party!

USE 4-ounce champagne glass

2 ounces apple juice
2 ounces ginger ale

Pour and serve.

Don't be surprised when your guests comment that it actually tastes like champagne. It does, but better.

FAUX PINK CHAMPAGNE

Refreshing as well as scintillating, for the most elegant of celebrations.

USE 4-ounce champagne glass
For each serving, combine in pitcher:
1 ounce cranberry juice
1 ounce apple juice
2 ounces ginger ale

Pour and serve.

Just a touch more tangy than Faux Champagne, with a perfect color.

FAUX CHABLIS

A clean, fruity taste that beautifully complements poultry or fish, and stands alone just as well.

USE 4-oz. wine glass
For each drink, combine in pitcher:
2 ounces white grape juice
2 ounces ginger ale

Pour and serve

Most tastes prefer faux wines chilled, unlike some traditional wines. However, you're free to experiment with individual preferences by serving at room temperature.

FAUX BORDEAUX

Rich and full-bodied, an all-juice faux wine that's perfect with pheasant or roast duck.

USE 4-ounce wine glass

For each serving, combine in pitcher:
2 ounces grape juice
2 ounces apple juice

Pour and serve.

FAUX ROSÉ

Rosé wine has found its greatest popularity in America. It's appropriate, then, that the flavor and color for this rosé mocktail should come from the all-American cranberry.

USE 4-ounce wine glass

For each serving, combine in pitcher:
2 ounces cranberry juice
2 ounces ginger ale

Pour and serve.

FAUX SPARKLING BURGUNDY

Rich grape flavor with a spicy effervescence. Perfect with meals.

USE 4-ounce wine glass

For each serving, combine in pitcher:
2 ounces grape juice
2 ounces ginger ale

Pour and serve.

FAUX PORT

An all-juice faux still wine, this robust flavor blends especially well with Italian food, beef or cheddar cheese.

USE 4-ounce wine glass

For each serving, combine in pitcher:
1½ ounces grape juice
1½ ounces apple juice
1 ounce cranberry juice

Pour and serve.

LEMON-WINE COOLER

A summery trick with de-alcoholized wine.

For about 20 servings, combine in punchbowl:

2 bottles de-alcoholized red or rosé wine, chilled
2-6 ounce cans frozen concentrated lemonade
1 quart club soda, chilled

Stir to blend, add ice cubes. Serve in punch cups or wineglasses. Garnish with lemon slices.

Chapter Four

◆

Traditionals

Chapter Four

◆

You drank some of these when you were younger; you drink some of them now. As a Mocktail bartender, you'll want to recognize these old standbys when somebody orders them. And somebody will! From the exotic Near Eastern Abdug to the all-American Virgin Mary, they've been at home in "mixed" company for a long time. Care has been taken to collect easy home variations of the recipes, with maximum taste appeal. Keep this chapter on hand, and you won't be stumped by the simple ones.

ABDUG

What to serve with exotic Eastern meals? Most Middle Eastern natives don't drink alcohol; this nutritious drink is one of their standbys, and provides your accompaniment to the spicy foods.

USE 10-ounce Collins glass

For each serving, combine in blender:
2 ounces plain yogurt
2 ounces water
1½ teaspoons dried mint

Blend 30 seconds or until smooth. Season with:
Salt, to taste.
Chill thoroughly and serve over ice.

For the Indian variation, called Lassi, add a little sugar and cardamom.

TWO TIMER'S COCKTAIL

A piquant combination of fruit and vegetable flavors.

USE 8-ounce Old-fashioned glass

For each serving, combine in cocktail shaker:
3 ounces tomato juice
3 ounces pineapple juice
dash lemon juice

Shake to blend, and pour over 2-3 ice cubes. Garnish with lemon wedge.

SARATOGA

Named for the famous mineral-water spa, this one carries a touch of elegance and sophistication.

USE 11-ounce highball glass

For each drink, stir in glass:
1 ounce lemon juice
½ teaspoon superfine sugar
¼ teaspoon Angostura bitters
Add:
3 ice cubes
6 ounces effervescent mineral water.

Serve plain or garnished with mint.

DIABOLO MENTHE

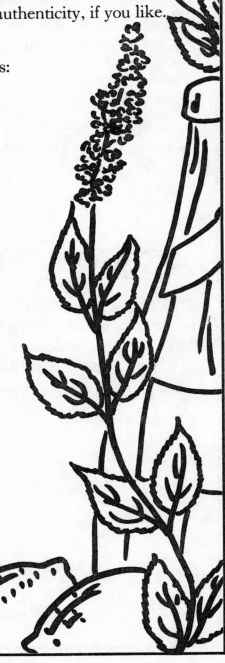

The new French craze. Make it with Perrier or another
"eau Francais" to emphasize the authenticity, if you like.

USE 10-ounce Collins glass

For each serving, combine in glass:
¼ lemon, squeezed
1 tablespoon creme de menthe syrup
1 tablespoon simple syrup
5 ounces sparkling water

Stir gently and serve. Garnish
with mint sprig.

HORSE'S NECK

A real classic, with "appeel."

USE 10-ounce highball or Collins glass
For each serving, combine in glass:
3 ice cubes
8 ounces ginger ale
1 whole lemon peel, spiral-cut

Hang the lemon peel in the ginger ale by one end, hooked on the rim of the glass. Add a lemon slice and serve.

ADAM'S ALE

Or Kitchen Spring, or Old Spigot, or any of a number of other fairly transparent nicknames, the drink of the ages. No calories, no caffeine, no sugar, no bubbles, it's equally classic in a silver goblet or a beggar's tin can.

USE 10-ounce frosted Collins glass or water goblet
Combine in glass:
3-4 ice cubes
Cold tap water

Serve with meals, or alone, but often.

PRAIRIE OYSTER

Originally intended as a "pick-me-up" for hangover sufferers, this drink has become quite popular. As a matter of medical fact, however, it can't do a thing for a hangover.

USE 4-6 ounce wineglass

For each serving, slip into glass:
1 unbroken egg yolk.
Add carefully:
1 teaspoon Worcestershire sauce
¼ teaspoon vinegar
1 dash Tabasco sauce
Salt and pepper

When drinking the Prairie Oyster, the egg yolk is to be swallowed whole.

ANGOSTURA COCKTAIL

Also known as Angostura Highball, this popular traditional Mocktail is outstanding for its sparkle and tang.

USE 10-ounce highball glass

3 ice cubes
1 teaspoon Angostura bitters
6 ounces ginger ale

Pour bitters over ice, fill with ginger ale, stir and serve.

CLUB COCKTAIL

One of the early bar mocktails, originally designed to look like an alcoholic drink.

USE 6-ounce Old-fashioned glass

For each serving, combine in glass:

2 sugar cubes
¼ teaspoon Angostura bitters
Whole lemon peel, spiral cut
2 cubes ice
5 ounces club soda

PARISETTE

Charming, wholesome, with a French accent.

USE 10-ounce Collins glass.

For 1 serving, combine in glass:

3 cubes ice
½ ounces grenadine syrup
6 ounces milk

Stir lightly and serve.

SHIRLEY TEMPLE

A perennial favorite; probably the queen of mocktails.

USE 11-ounce Collins glass
For each serving, combine in pitcher:
1 ounce grenadine
6 ounces ginger ale

Pour over ice, serve garnished with maraschino cherry and orange slice.

Shirley says she doesn't like it, but what does she know?

ROY ROGERS

Remember Ol' Roy riding into the sunset? Maybe you remember when the restaurants served this one to young cowboys, while the girls had a Shirley Temple.

USE 11-ounce Collins glass
For each drink, pour gently over ice:
½ ounce grenadine
2 ounces orange juice
6 ounces ginger ale

Serve with maraschino cherry impaled on a straw, without stirring.

RASPBERRY VINEGAR

This recipe, from the turn of the century (perhaps earlier) takes time to prepare and is bottled ahead of serving time. It was apparently one of the early soft drinks.

For each batch of syrup, use:
12 pounds ripe strawberries
3 quarts cider vinegar

Pour one-third of the vinegar over one-third of the berries. Let stand 3 days. Drain off and save juice. Strain berries through cheesecloth. Save liquid.

Repeat procedure with another quart of vinegar and another one-third of the berries. Add resulting juice to first batch. Repeat with remainder of berries and vinegar.

Measure juice and add:
1 pound sugar per quart of juice
Boil for 5 minutes; bottle.

Serve over ice, mixed with equal portions of club soda. Sweeten further if desired.

SOBER OX

For those who like the solid taste of beef.

USE 6-ounce Old-fashioned glass
For each drink, combine in glass:
2-3 ice cubes
3 ounces chilled beef bouillon

Stir gently. Serve garnished with lemon wedge.

BEEFY BRACER

Just-right accompaniment to a summer brunch, or in smaller portions, with a winter breakfast.

USE 10-ounce highball glass

For 6 servings, combine in pitcher:
2 quarts spicy hot vegetable cocktail juice
2 10-½ ounce cans condensed beef broth
1 dash garlic powder

Stir with ice, serve garnished with lemon slices

VARIOUS VIRGINS

Tomato juice combines easily with a wide variety of flavors. Here are a few combinations, and you can create your own "stars" for a breakfast or brunch performance, or anytime.

VIRGIN MARIE

For each serving, combine in pitcher:

3 ounces tomato juice
2 ounces club soda
2 ice cubes
1 dash Worcestershire sauce
½ ounce lemon juice
Salt and pepper to taste

Serve over ice, with a celery stick.

VIRGIN MARIA

For each serving, combine in blender:

4 ounces tomato juice
½ can peeled chili
1 dash lemon juice
2 ice cubes

Blend until smooth on high speed. Serve over ice, garnished with lemon slice.

MONA LISA

For each serving, combine
in blender:

3 ounces tomato juice
3 ounces zucchini, cut small
1 very thin *slice onion*
1 dash Italian Seasoning
2 ice cubes

Blend at high speed until smooth. Serve over ice.

VIRGIN MARY

Non-alcoholic sister to the Bloody Mary, this one has
become something of a celebrity in its own right.

USE 8-ounce Old-fashioned glass
For each serving, combine in cocktail shaker:

4 ounces tomato juice
½ ounce lemon juice
1 teaspoon catsup
1 dash Worcestershire sauce
1 dash celery salt
1 dash Tabasco sauce
Freshly ground pepper, to taste
3 ice cubes

Shake vigorously and strain
into glass. Garnish
with lemon slice
or celery stick.

CLAM JUICE COCKTAIL

In old movies, this was a standard morning pick-me-up for people who'd been partying late, and woke up in luxurious, but strange, places. It works just as well for holiday breakfasts and luncheons.

USE 6-ounce juice or Old-fashioned glass

For each serving, combine in cocktail shaker:

1 teaspoon catsup
1 dash celery salt
1 or 2 dashes tabasco sauce
5 ounces clam juice
2 ice cubes

Shake and strain. Serve garnished with lemon wedge.

SASSY JUICE

For each serving, combine in cocktail shaker:

4 oz. tomato juice
1 dash tabasco sauce

Shake thoroughly and pour over ice.

TOMATO-
CARROT JUICE

For each serving, combine in blender:

3 ounces tomato juice
3 ounces carrots, thinly sliced
1 ice cube
dash horseradish

Blend at high speed until smooth. Season with salt and pepper to taste. Serve over ice.

MORNING AFTER

For each serving, combine in blender:

3 ounces tomato juice
1 egg
2 ice cubes
½ teaspoon horseradish
½ teaspoon lemon juice

Blend 30 seconds. Sprinkle with celery salt.

C-SHARP

3 ounces mixed vegetable (V-8) juice
½ teaspoon lemon juice
½ teaspoon lime juice

Stir thoroughly and serve over ice.

SHRINKING VIOLET

Another old-fashioned favorite that will remind Grandpa of his boyhood.

USE 11-ounce Collins glass

For each serving, combine in pitcher:
6 ounces lemonade (see recipe)
1 ounce grape juice

Pour over ice, serve garnished with lemon slice or small cluster of fresh grapes.

NOEL COWARD

The refreshing favorite drink of a famous sophisticate.

USE 8-ounce highball glass
For 1 serving, combine in glass:
2 ice cubes
6 ounces Perrier water
1 lime wedge

Very simple, and one of the most popular traditionals.

PRISM

Not exactly a pousse-café, but quite pretty.

USE 4-ounce parfait glass
For each serving, fill glass with crushed ice.
Add:
½ ounce grenadine
2 ounces ginger ale (more if needed to cover ice)
Float on top:
½ ounce Rose's Lime Juice

Serve without stirring.

RUM AND COKE: HOLD THE RUM

Okay, everybody knows how to serve this. Just don't be surprised when it's ordered this way. Good luck on avoiding the cola controversies, ranging from brand preference to formula preference. To be on the safe side, serve in unmarked bottles!

USE 11-ounce highball glass
For each serving, combine in glass:
3-4 ice cubes
6 ounces cola

CAFÉ AU LAIT

The elegant French coffee you always find in romance and mystery novels.

USE standard coffee cups.
For two servings, prepare:
1 cup freshly brewed coffee
1 cup scalded rich milk
Pour coffee and milk simultaneously into each cup.

For Viennese Coffee, substitute whipped cream for milk.

ICED MEXICAN COFFEE

Spicy and elegant; sure to please coffee lovers.

USE 10-ounce Collins glasses

For 4 servings, combine in pitcher:
1 stick cinnamon
1 quart double-strength coffee
Steep 2 hours. Combine in separate container:
2 ounces boiling water
1 teaspoon instant coffee
When coffee is dissolved, add:
6 ounces simple syrup
Remove cinnamon from pitcher, stir in:
4 ounces heavy cream
Instant coffee mixture to taste

Serve over ice, garnished with whipped-cream.

BLACK AND TAN

A 50's favorite. You may remember it from the comedy, "Laverne and Shirley."

USE 10-ounce highball glass

For each serving, combine in glass:
3 ice cubes
4 ounces cola
2 ounces milk

Stir gently and serve.

LEMONADE

Made in the shade, stirred with a spade, by a pretty maid, as the old verse goes. Reminiscent of gazebos and handlebar moustaches, picnics and Fourth-of-July band concerts.

USE decorated paper cups
Combine in pitcher:
Juice and spent shells of 3 lemons
1 quart water
8 ounces superfine sugar

Stir and serve over ice.

PINK LEMONADE

A garden-party necessity in all the old storybooks.

USE 10-ounce highball glass
6 ounces lemonade (see recipe)
½ ounce grenadine or maraschino syrup

Serve over ice, garnished with a maraschino cherry.

LIMEADE

The kind they used to serve in the corner drugstore.

USE 11-ounce Collins glass
For each serving, combine in pitcher:
Juice and spent shell of ½ lime
1½ ounces simple syrup
6 ounces club soda

Stir gently and pour over ice. Be sure each glass gets a lime shell.

LEMON SODA

Serve it on your front lawn after returning from an outdoor concert, while you watch the fireflies and listen to the crickets.

USE 10-ounce stemmed water goblet, or Collins glass.
For each serving, combine in glass:
1 tablespoon vanilla ice cream
1 ounce frozen lemonade concentrate
Stir to blend. Add:
4 ounces cold milk
4 ounces ginger ale
1 scoop vanilla ice cream

Serve with straw and long-handled spoon. Garnish with lemon slice.

GINGER ICE COOLER

Great refreshment for a summer-afternoon get-together.

USE 10-ounce Collins glasses

Freeze ginger ale ahead of time in ice cube trays, to make ginger ice.

Combine in pitcher:

6 ounces frozen lemonade or limeade concentrate

8 ounces simple syrup

Stir together well, and add:

1 quart ginger ale

Pour over ginger ice in glasses and serve.

HAWAIIAN ORANGE JUICE

Good old O.J., with a Polynesian accent.

USE 8-ounce tumbler or water goblet

For each serving, combine in blender:

1 slice canned pineapple

6 ounces orange juice

1 dash lemon juice

Blend 30 seconds, serve over ice and garnish with pineapple stick.

BANANA-LIME LIMBO

A "show-off" specialty from the Virgin Islands.

USE 10-ounce Collins glass
For each serving, combine in blender:
1½ ounces Rose's Lime Juice
½ large, ripe banana
2 cubes ice
2 ounces confectioner's sugar

Blend at high speed 60 seconds. Pour over ice. Serve garnished with lime slice.

CHOCOLATE SODA

A delicious dessert-beverage, it's just right with a sandwich for lunch.

USE 10-ounce stemmed water goblet
For each serving, combine in glass:
1 small scoop chocolate ice cream
1½ ounces chocolate syrup
Blend together and add:
4 ounces cold milk
4 ounces sparkling water
Float on top:
1 scoop chocolate ice cream

Garnish with whipped cream and cherry. Serve with straw and long-handled spoon.

STRAWBERRY SODA

Another beauty from the old drugstore days.

USE 10-ounce stemmed water goblet.

For each serving, liquefy in blender:

2 ounces fresh or frozen strawberries
1½ ounces simple syrup

Pour in glass, and add:

4 ounces cold milk
4 ounces club soda
1 scoop strawberry ice cream.

Top with sweetened whipped cream and maraschino cherry or fresh strawberry. Serve with straw and long spoon.

BLACK COW

Stirs up memories of the gay ninties, knickers, Gibson girls and ice-cream parlors.

USE 11-ounce Collins glass
For each serving, pour in glass:
6 ounces sarsaparilla
Add:
1 scoop vanilla ice cream

Stir and serve.

CHOCOLATE MILK SHAKE

No list of favorite drinks would be complete without this all-time great.

USE 10-ounce highball glass
For each serving, combine in cocktail shaker:
2 scoops chocolate ice cream or ice milk
2 ounces chocolate syrup
8 ounces cold milk
Shake to desired thickness and serve.

The thicker shakes, usually made with ice milk or soft ice cream, are often prepared in the South, while Northern palates like the milk shake or "frappe" made with ice cream and blended to a thin, smooth consistency.

HOT GRAPEFRUIT TODDY

A little tropical sunlight for a cold day.

USE 6-ounce Old-fashioned glasses or coffee mugs

For 8 servings, combine in saucepan:

1½ quarts grapefruit juice
1½ ounces sugar
1 cinnamon stick
1 teaspoon cloves

Heat slowly; DO NOT BOIL. Pour and serve sprinkled lightly with ground cinnamon.

HOT CHOCOLATE

The perennial reliable; warms the body from the inside out. Inca royalty would have envied us its availability and ease of preparation.

USE standard coffee or cocoa mug

For each serving, combine in mug:

1 heaping teaspoon cocoa
2 heaping teaspoons sugar
1 dash salt
2 teaspoons milk
Stir until smooth and add:
8 ounces milk, heated. DO NOT BOIL.

Stir to blend, and serve with whipped cream or marshmallows.

HOT SPICED CIDER

For Hallowe'en, football and all the other fall festivities.

USE 6-ounce coffee mugs

For 5 servings, combine in heavy saucepan:

1 quart unfermented cider
2 ounces superfine sugar
1 cinnamon stick
¼ teaspoon whole allspice
½ teaspoon whole cloves

Heat to boiling, remove and let stand for 3 hours. Reheat, pour into mugs and serve.

MEXICAN CHOCOLATE

A treat fit for the ancient Aztec gods.

USE standard teacups or coffee mugs

For 4-6 servings, combine in blender:

1 quart Hot Chocolate (see recipe)
1 teaspoon ground cinnamon
1 dash allspice
1 teaspoon vanilla

Blend until frothy. Serve topped with:

Sweetened whipped cream

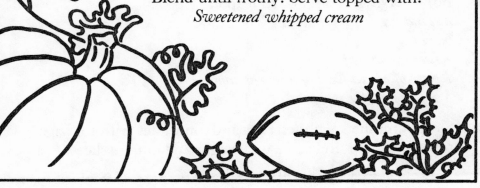

TEA

A panacea recognized by medical science for its tension-relieving, energizing qualities. Make it the easy way with teabags, one cup at a time, or use the traditional method.

HOT TEA

USE china teapot and teacups.

Fill teapot with boiling water and empty, to heat.
For each cup of tea, combine in pot:
1 rounded teaspoon loose tea or 1 tea bag
1 cup fresh boiling water

Steep 5 minutes; remove tea bags or strain tea and pour.

HOT GINGER TEA

Your great-grandmother used to serve this to ladies' meetings. Great-granddad didn't know what he was missing.

USE standard teacups
For 4 servings, combine in teapot:
2 standard or 1 "family size" tea bags
6 cloves
1 stick cinnamon
1 piece of crystallized ginger, cut small
3 cups boiling water

Steep 3 minutes with tea bags and 5 minutes with tea bags removed. Pour and serve with sugar and orange slices.

RUSSIAN TEA

A lovely old-world accompaniment to dessert. There are many variations of this recipe; this one is really from Russia.

USE china teapot and cups.

For six servings, combine in saucepan:
1 quart water
1 stick cinnamon
5 whole cloves
4 ounces sugar
Stir over heat until sugar dissolves. Turn heat higher until mixture boils.
In preheated teapot (which has been filled with boiling water and emptied) combine:
2 rounded teaspoons tea (or 2 tea bags)
½ orange peel, cut in strips
Spice-water mixture
Steep five minutes, strain and return to teapot. Add:
6 ounces heated orange juice

Serve with slices of lemon.

ICED TEA

A southern favorite now popular nationwide.

Brew as for HOT TEA but use 3 rounded teaspoons loose tea or 3 tea bags for each 1½ cups boiling water.
After steeping, allow to cool 2-3 hours without refrigeration.

Pour over ice in tall glasses. Serve with lemon or mint leaves.

CAFÉ L'ORANGE

A special treat for coffee lovers.

USE standard coffee cups.

For 4 servings, combine in coffeepot
1 orange, sliced and studded with:
Whole cloves (4 in each slice)

Pour coffee over oranges and steep 30 minutes. Remove orange slices and cloves. Reheat coffee and serve garnished with sweetened whipped cream or cinnamon.

Chapter Five

◆

Phabulous
Phonies

Chapter Five

◆

Sometimes, just leaving the liquor out of a popular mixed drink will result in a tasty non-alcoholic version. Sometimes, though, the product of this procedure will fall flat, or worse, be an absolute disaster. So if you're inclined to experiment, use yourself or your family as the guinea pig, *before* the party starts. Nobody will get drunk from testing the recipes.

On the other hand, if you like your formula pre-measured and pre-tested, the pages in this chapter will be just what you're looking for. These "phonies" are all non-alcoholic copycats of some of the best known characters in the bar.

MOCQUIRI

Yes, it's a "mock Daiquiri." Light and refreshing.

USE 5-ounce Cocktail glass, frosted

For each serving, combine in blender:

2 ice cubes
4 ounces apple juice
½ teaspoon lime juice
½ teaspoon lemon juice
1 teaspoon confectioner's sugar

Blend 25 seconds. Serve garnished with lime slice.

For a Mockardi, or mock Bacardi, add ½ ounce grenadine before blending.

JOE COLLINS

Heard of John Collins and Tom Collins? This is the brother who drives them home after a party.

USE 11-ounce Collins glass

For each serving, combine in glass:
2 rounded teaspoons confectioner's sugar
½ ounce lemon juice
Stir together and add:
3 ice cubes
6 ounces soda

Stir and serve garnished with lemon slice.

It's a well-known fact that some people have been drinking "Collins mix on the rocks" for years. The pre-mix can be an acceptable shortcut.

HARVEY'S BROTHER

Keeps the family tradition with a lighter touch.

USE 8-ounce highball glass

For each serving, combine in pitcher:
2 ounces lemon-lime soda
5 ounces orange juice
½ to ¾ teaspoon anise extract

Stir and serve over 4-5 ice cubes.

PILGRIM FATHER

For those who like an especially tart drink.

USE 8-ounce highball glass
For two servings, combine in pitcher:
7 ounces cranberry juice
½ teaspoon fresh lime juice
2 ounces club soda or effervescent mineral water
2 teaspoons superfine sugar

Stir, pour in ice-filled glasses and serve.

PILGRIM MOTHER

A little sweeter than the Pilgrim Father, but in the same New England tradition.

USE 11-ounce Collins glass
For each serving, combine in glass:
3 ice cubes
3 ounces cranberry juice
2 ounces ginger ale
3 ounces orange juice

Stir gently, serve garnished with orange slice.

METHODIST PRESBYTERIAN

Try this one to fool a friend.

USE 10-ounce Collins glass
For 1 serving, combine in glass:
¼ teaspoon rum extract
1 teaspoon molasses
4 ounces ginger ale
Stir to dissolve molasses, and add:
4 ounces club soda
2 ice cubes

Stir and serve garnished with lemon slice.

NAKED LADY

A hint of passion, and a tangy tartness that's definitely
 R-rated. (for Refreshing)

USE 5-ounce cocktail glass
For each serving, combine in blender:
3 ice cubes
2 ounces Wink
½ ounce passionfruit syrup
¼ ounce lime juice
½ lemon juice

Blend 30 seconds. Serve garnished with two maraschino
cherries.

FRUIT MOCQUIRI

Delicious in any flavor, but heavenly with strawberries.

USE 4-ounce cocktail glass.

For two servings, combine in blender:
3 ice cubes
4 ounces strawberries, peaches, bananas or other fruit.
½ teaspoon lime juice
1 teaspoon confectioner's sugar
4 ounces lemon-lime soda

Blend 30 seconds, pour and serve garnished with
strawberry, peach slice, lime slice or other appropriate fruit.

KATYDID

Related to a grasshopper, but can sing all night without ever getting off-key.

USE 4-ounce cocktail glass

For each serving, combine in blender:
4 ice cubes
2 ounces light cream
½ ounce cream of coconut
1 ounce non-alcoholic creme de menthe syrup
1 drop green vegetable coloring

Blend 25 seconds; pour and serve.

COLA LIBRE

A real tongue-tingler.

USE 10-ounce Collins glass.

For one serving, combine carefully in glass:
½ ounce lime juice
3 ice cubes
6 ounces cola

Serve garnished with lime slice.

GINGER BUCK

A straightforward refresher.

USE 11-ounce Collins glass
For each serving, combine in pitcher:
½ ounce lemon juice
1 ounce simple syrup
6 ounces ginger ale

Stir and serve over 3-4 ice cubes. Garnish with lemon slice.

GINGER JULEP

If the old Kentucky colonels spin in their graves, let them.
It's good for the soil.

USE 8-ounce highball glass
For one serving, muddle in glass:
4 mint leaves. Add:
½ ounce non-alcoholic creme de menthe syrup
½ teaspoon fresh lemon juice
3 ounces cracked ice
5 ounces ginger ale

Stir gently. Garnish with sprig of fresh mint.

PEREGRINE FALCON

Combines smoothness and sunshine, like an early-morning flight. If you're the pilot, this drink won't ground you.

USE 6-ounce Old-fashioned glass

For each serving, combine in shaker:

2 ounces apple juice or unfermented cider
1½ ounces grapefruit juice
½ ounce simple syrup
2 ice cubes

Shake vigorously, pour and serve.

SOBER SUNRISE

Every bit as pretty as the Mexican sunrises, and a lot easier on the head.

USE 11-ounce Collins glass

For each serving, combine in blender:

3 ice cubes
3 ounces orange juice
1 rounded teaspoon confectioner's sugar
6 ounces Wink

Blend 30 seconds, pour into glass over:

½ ounce grenadine syrup

Serve garnished with orange slice.

PIÑA CON NADA

In case your Spanish is rusty, "Con Nada" means "with nothing." This variation has already begun to catch on, and a taste will tell you why.

USE 5½-ounce cocktail glass

For two servings, combine in blender:

5 ounces ice
3 ounces pineapple juice
1 ounce cream of coconut
1 rounded teaspoon confectioner's sugar.

Blend 20-30 seconds. Serve garnished with lemon or lime peel or pineapple stick.

UNSCREW

To loosen up without getting tight, this is the tool to use.

USE 11-ounce Collins glass
For each serving, combine in pitcher:
4 ounces orange juice
4 ounces lemon-lime soda

Pour over 3-4 ice cubes and garnish with orange slice.

SAFEDRIVER

One of two alcohol-free variations of the Screwdriver.

USE 11-ounce Collins glass
For each serving, combine in pitcher:
4 ounces orange juice
4 ounces ginger ale

Stir and pour over 3-4 ice cubes to serve.

GIMMEIT

Looks for all the world like a gimlet, but with a difference.

USE 4-ounce cocktail glass, frosted
For each serving, combine in glass:
4 ounces chilled ginger ale
1 teaspoon Rose's Lime Juice

Stir once and serve garnished with lime wedge.

GREEN ANGEL

A saintly sparkler.

USE 4-ounce cocktail glass.
For each serving, combine in pitcher:
3 ounces lemon-lime soda
2 teaspoons creme de menthe
1 teaspoon lime juice
5-6 drops Angostura bitters

Stir and pour. Garnish with lime wedge.

BUNNYTAIL

Puts a hop in your step without giving you a pink nose.

USE 6-ounce Old-fashioned glass
For each serving, combine in cocktail shaker:
3 ounces apple juice or sweet cider
1 ounce orange juice
½ ounce lemon juice
2 teaspoons maple syrup
3 ice cubes

Shake vigorously, pour and serve.

LOCOMOTIVE

Powerful taste treat.

USE 10-ounce stemmed water goblet
For each serving, combine in cocktail shaker:
3 ounces white grape juice
2 ounces ginger ale
2 ounces pineapple juice
3 ice cubes

Shake vigorously, pour and serve garnished with a pineapple stick.

WHIPPET

Custom-tailor this one by making it with your guest's favorite sparkling water, or use your own favorite club soda.

USE 8-ounce highball glass
For each serving, combine in glass:
2 ice cubes
3 ounces grapefruit juice
3 ounces effervescent mineral water

Stir gently and serve.

MIAMI

A kiss of the famous Florida sunshine,
with its own élan.

USE 6-ounce cocktail glass

For each serving, combine in
cocktail shaker:
1 ounce grapefruit juice
2 ounces Collins mix
2 teaspoons maraschino syrup
4 ounces crushed ice

Shake vigorously, strain and serve.

CHERRY SPIN

A friendly drink, easy to make
and refreshing.

USE 5-ounce cocktail glass

For each serving, combine in
cocktail shaker:
¼ ounce lime juice
3 ounces Wink
½ ounce maraschino syrup
2 ice cubes

Shake thoroughly, pour and serve
garnished with
maraschino cherry.

SHASTA DAISY

Sparkles with sophistication.

USE 8-ounce water goblet

For each serving, combine in pitcher:

1 ounce raspberry syrup, or ½ ounce juice from canned red
raspberries, and 1 ounce simple syrup
1 teaspoon lemon juice
¼ teaspoon artificial rum flavoring
2 ounces club soda

Stir and pour into glass which has been half-filled with crushed ice. Garnish with raspberries, pineapple stick or mint sprig.

PINK PRINCESS

Something like a Pink Lady, but definitely regal.

USE 5½-ounce cocktail glass, sugar-frosted

For each serving, combine in blender:

1 ounce light cream
1 ounce confectioner's sugar
1 teaspoon grenadine
Blend 10 seconds. Add:
2 ounces ice
3 ounces lemon-lime soda

Blend 20 more seconds. Pour and serve.

CLOVER BLOSSOM

Fresh and frothy. Reminds you of watching clouds on a warm spring day.

USE 8-ounce water goblet
For each serving, combine in cocktail shaker:
3 ounces lemon-lime soda
½ ounce lemon juice
1 egg white
½ ounce grenadine
8 drops Angostura bitters
2 tsp. simple syrup
2 ice cubes

Shake well, pour and serve garnished with real clover blossom floating on top.

MOSQUITO

This is one you definitely *won't* want to avoid on a warm summer evening.

USE 10-ounce Collins glass
For each serving, combine in glass:
3 ice cubes
1 serving Limeade (See Recipe)
1 teaspoon creme de menthe syrup

LAVENDER

An old-fashioned flavor with a bright sparkle.

USE 8-ounce Old-fashioned glass

For each serving, combine in pitcher:
3 ounces grape juice
½ ounce lemon juice
½ ounce simple syrup
3 ounces club soda

Stir gently, pour and serve garnished with a lemon slice.

COCONUT ROSE

Too good to pass up, and it shows.

USE 6-ounce water goblet

For each serving, combine in shaker:
2 ounces lemon-lime soda
¼ ounce cream of coconut
¼ lemon juice
¼ ounce maraschino syrup
3 ice cubes

Shake vigorously, pour and serve.

ROSE GARDEN

Delicate, elegant and sophisticated. A real pleaser.

USE 5-ounce cocktail glass

For each serving, combine in cocktail shaker:
1½ ounces white grape juice
1½ ounces club soda
1 teaspoon grenadine
1 teaspoon lemon juice
1 egg white
3 ounces ice
½ ounce confectioner's sugar
Shake vigorously. Add:
1 teaspoon cream

Continue shaking to blend. Strain into glass and sprinkle with cinnamon.

RUN FOR THE ROSES

An alternative to the traditional (or non-traditional) julep for a Derby Day celebration

USE 6-ounce Old-fashioned glass, sugar-frosted

For each serving, combine in shaker:
2 ounces Collins mix
1 teaspoon lemon juice
1 ounce pineapple juice
½ ounce maraschino syrup
3 ice cubes

Shake and strain into glass. Serve garnished with lemon slice.

BLUE LAGOON

Beautiful and exotic, like the mysteries of a tropical island.

USE 10-ounce stemmed glass
For each serving, combine in blender:
5 cubes ice
1 ounce lemon juice
1 ounce pineapple juice
2 ounces confectioner's sugar
½ teaspoon mint extract
2½ ounces lemon-lime soda
3 drops blue vegetable coloring

Blend 20-30 seconds. Serve garnished with pineapple stick
or lemon slice.

ALOHA

Dream of Hawaii — a luau, a smiling dancer, the sounds of
surf and native drums. This is the drink you're holding.

USE chilled, sugar-rimmed champagne glass
For each serving, combine in cocktail shaker:
1 ounce pineapple juice
½ Rose's Lime Juice
1 ounce cream of coconut
1 ounce soda
2 ice cubes

Shake well with ice. Pour and serve garnished with
pineapple stick.

ISLAND PARADISE

Reminiscent of steel-drum bands, bright birds and jungle flowers. The magic is delicious taste, not voodoo.

USE sugar-frosted champagne glasses
For each serving, combine in blender:
1 ounce orange juice
1 ounce cream of coconut
1 ounce lime juice
½ teaspoon simple syrup
3 ice cubes
¼ ounce lemon juice

Blend 30 seconds at high speed. Pour and serve. May be garnished with paper umbrella.

TAHITIAN CRUISE

Colorful and fruity. Perfect for a summer afternoon.

USE 5½-ounce Old-fashioned glass
For two servings, combine in blender:
3 ice cubes
3 ounces lemon-lime soda
¼ ounce Rose's Lime Juice
1 ounce pineapple juice
½ ounce grenadine
½ ounce simple syrup

Blend 30 seconds. Strain and serve garnished with orange slice.

KAMEHAMEHA

Served in a fresh pineapple which has been hollowed out, this one looks just like the exotic drinks on the TV shows, and it's as proud as its name.

USE pineapple with top cut off and hollowed, or 8-ounce water goblet.

For each serving, combine in cocktail shaker:
3 ice cubes
1½ ounces lemon-lime soda
1½ ounces pineapple juice
1 ounce grape juice
1 teaspoon simple syrup

Shake vigorously, pour and serve with a royal flourish.

NATIVE GIRL

A tropical beauty with an innocent blush.

USE 4-ounce cocktail glass, frosted
For each serving, combine in shaker:
2 ounces cream of coconut
1 ounce cream
½ ounce grenadine
½ ounce Rose's Lime Juice
3 ice cubes

Shake vigorously, strain and serve.

DRAGON LADY

Enticing and festive.

USE 4-ounce cocktail glass

For each serving, combine in glass:
1 teaspoon creme de menthe syrup
3 ounces lemon-lime soda
2 ice cubes

Stir and serve garnished with mint sprig.

STRAWBERRY CON NADA

Made with a delicious new mix; easy and satisfying.

USE 6-ounce glass

For each serving, combine in blender:
1 ounce Strawberry Colada mix
2 ounces ginger ale
3 ice cubes

Blend 30 seconds and serve. Garnish with a whole strawberry.

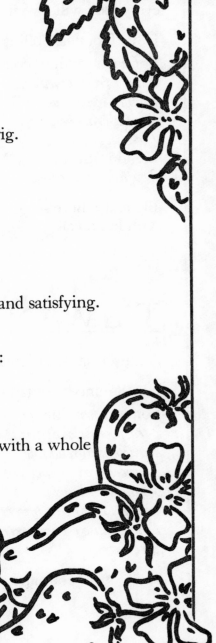

LUAU LEMONADE

Nobody's going to believe there's no lemon in it, but everybody will love it.

USE 10-ounce Collins glass

For each serving, combine in blender:
2 slices fresh pineapple
1 ounce confectioner's sugar
½ ounce raspberry syrup (or juice from canned red raspberries.)
1 ice cube
Blend until smooth. Add:
2 ounces club soda

Blend 10 more seconds, pour and serve over ice, garnished with lemon slice.

TAIWAN

An inscrutable Oriental delight.

USE 8-ounce cocktail glass

For each serving, combine in cocktail shaker:
2 teaspoons Passionfruit syrup
2 teaspoons grenadine
2 ounces orange juice
3 ounces club soda
1 dash Angostura bitters
1 dash anise cooking extract
3 ice cubes

Shake well, pour and serve.

WAHINE

Imagine blue sky, blue water and this blue delicacy served with a Polynesian smile.

USE 5-ounce water goblet or cocktail glass

For two servings, combine in blender:
1 ounce lemon juice
1 ounce pineapple juice
3 ounces confectioner's sugar
½ teaspoon rum flavoring
2½ ounces lemon-lime soda
5 ounces ice
3 drops blue vegetable coloring

Blend 30 seconds. Garnish with pineapple stick or small orchid.

PRINCE ALPHONSE

This is what King Alphonse was like before he got old and fermented.

USE 1-ounce cordial glass

For one serving, pour in glass:
½ ounce non-alcoholic creme de cocoa sauce
Pour gently on top, over back of spoon:
½ ounce heavy cream (slight less than a full ½ ounce, in order to serve without spilling.)

ROSE MARIE

Mellow as the old-fashioned song of the same name.

USE 8-ounce highball glass

For each serving, combine in shaker:
3 ounces apple juice or sweet cider
¾ ounce lime juice
1 ounce grenadine
3 ice cubes

Shake vigorously and serve garnished with a maraschino cherry.

PUERTO RICAN PRINCESS

A touch of artificial rum flavoring gives this pink beauty that "Are you sure?" taste.

USE sugar-frosted champagne glass
For each serving, combine in blender:
½ egg white
3 teaspoons Rose's Lime Juice
2 teaspoons grenadine
3 ice cubes
2 ounces lemon-lime soda
4 teaspoons confectioner's sugar
½ teaspoon artificial rum-flavored cooking extract

Blend 30 seconds, pour and serve.

CHIQUITITA

Exotic and beautiful. A tropical delight.

USE 5-ounce cocktail or champagne glasses.
For two servings, combine in blender:
1 banana
2 ounces orange juice
2 ounces light cream
1 ounce grenadine
3 ice cubes

Blend 30 seconds. Pour and serve. Garnish with orange slice or paper umbrella.

RUSSIAN DEFECTOR

A rich, delicious mocha drink. Similar to a White Russian, but without the "Russian."

USE Manhattan or rocks glass

For two servings, combine in small container:
1 teaspoon instant coffee
2 ounces boiling water
Refrigerate until cool. Combine in glass with:
2 ounces chocolate syrup
4 ounces milk
Stir to blend. Top generously with:
Sweetened whipped cream

COCOMINT

A luscious "dessert drink" with a combination of old-fashioned favorite flavors.

USE 10-ounce stemmed glass or two 4-ounce glasses

For one large or two small servings, combine in blender or cocktail shaker:
1 scoop chocolate ice cream
1 ounce cream of coconut
¼ teaspoon mint extract
6 ounces club soda

Blend or shake as desired. Blended drinks will be smoother, shaken drink thicker. Serve garnished with mint sprig.

Chapter Six

◆

New
Faces

Chapter Six

◆

These "original" recipes combine new and unusual flavor ideas with some combinations that have been around for a while, but tested and measured recipes haven't been readily available.

Some of the combinations are surprising. The Alligator, for instance, looks formidable, but if you have the courage to try it, you may never voluntarily drink plain grapefruit juice again. Other recipes, though, are so good you can almost taste them when you read the recipe.

If this chapter wakes up your imagination as well as your taste, go ahead — have fun creating your own "secret" formula that pops eyeballs. After all, originality is what makes a party succeed.

PRINCESS DI

Delicious hot or iced, a fitting tribute to a lovely young woman.

USE standard teacups or tall glasses

For four servings iced, or 8 servings hot, combine in pitcher or large teapot:

1 quart freshly brewed TEA (see recipe)
4 ounces superfine sugar
1 lime, cut in quarters and squeezed into tea
1 teaspoon mint extract

Stir and serve fresh, in cups or over ice.

ASTRONAUT

The kids will love it!

USE 10-ounce Collins glass
For each serving, combine in pitcher:
1 ounce Tang
6 ounces Club Soda

Serve over ice.

EAST AND WEST

An All-American appetizer.

USE 4-ounce tumbler or winestem
For each serving, combine in pitcher:
2 ounces cranberry juice
2 ounces pineapple juice

Stir and pour.

MINT LEMONADE

Cool, refreshing, with a new twist to a favorite tradition.

USE 10-ounce Collins glass
For each serving, combine in pitcher:
6 ounces LEMONADE (see recipe)
½ ounce creme de menthe syrup

Stir, pour over 3 ice cubes. Serve garnished with mint sprig
and lemon slice.

SPACE SHUTTLE

An Astronaut with a different personality.

USE 10-ounce Collins glass
For each serving, combine in blender:
3 ice cubes
3 rounded teaspoons Tang
6 ounces club soda

Blend 25 seconds or until slushy. Serve garnished with orange slice.

MOONBEAM

A taste of crisp New England winter nights.

USE 8-ounce Old-fashioned glass, frosted
For each serving, combine in blender:
6 ounces chilled white grape juice
½ egg white
2 teaspoons maple syrup

Blend 20-25 seconds. Pour and serve.

GLACIER

Icy-cool, fresh and inviting.

USE 4-ounce winestem or champagne glass
For two servings, combine in blender:
5 ice cubes
6 ounces lemon-lime soda
¼ teaspoon mint cooking extract
¼ teaspoon anise cooking extract
2 drops blue vegetable coloring
½ ounce confectioner's sugar
Blend 30 seconds; serve garnished with mint leaf.

ANNIE SUNSHINE

Probably the most thirst-quenching drink you can imagine.
Easy and good for you.

USE 4-ounce juice glass
For each serving, combine in pitcher:
2 ounces orange juice
2 ounces apple juice

Stir thoroughly and serve.

For a refresher after strenuous sports, you'll want bigger
servings.

FUSCHIA

A sweet sparkler.

USE 4-ounce champagne glass

For each serving, combine in glass:
2 ounces grape juice
2 ounces club soda
1 teaspoon grenadine

Squeeze in juice of ¼ fresh lime. Drop shell in glass.

ROYAL PURPLE

Just a touch of tang to a fine old classic.

USE 6-ounce glass

For each serving, combine in glass:
6 ounces chilled grape juice
juice of ¼ lemon

Stir. Garnish with lemon wedge.

SPIRIT HOPPER

Two old friends join for a new point of view.

USE 10-ounce Highball glass
For each serving, combine in pitcher:
4 ounces cola
4 ounces lemon-lime soda

Stir and pour over ice. Serve with straw.

MOTORCYCLE

Add a tingly taste by combining old favorites.

USE 10-ounce Collins glass
For each serving, combine in pitcher:
3 ounces cola
3 ounces ginger ale

Stir, pour over 3 ice cubes in glass and serve.

ALLIGATOR

You won't believe it till you taste it.

USE 4-ounce juice glass
For each serving, combine in pitcher:
3 ounces grapefruit juice
Juice of ¼ fresh lime

Stir well. Serve garnished with thin strip of lime peel.

CROCODILE

A relative of the Alligator, found in different waters.

USE 8-ounce glass

For each serving, combine in pitcher:
3 ounces grapefruit juice
3 ounces club soda
1 teaspoon Rose's Lime Juice
½ ounce simple syrup

Stir gently and pour over 3-4 ice cubes.
Garnish with lime slice.

SUICIDE

An old idea that's unique with every drink. Usually favored by those under age 15.

USE 10-ounce tumbler

For each serving, combine in glass:
3 ice cubes
1 ounce each of any six different soft drinks

Stir and serve with straw.

ORAMATO

Especially for vitamin-C fans.

USE 4-ounce juice glass
For each serving, combine in pitcher:
1 ounce chilled tomato juice
2 ounces orange juice

Keep well chilled. Serve over ice cube.

JASMINE

Fluffy, flavorful and definitely spring.

USE 10-ounce Collins glass
For each serving, combine in blender:
1 cup strawberries
6 ounces pineapple juice
½ egg white
½ ounce simple syrup or honey

Blend 20 seconds or until smooth and frothy.
Garnish with pineapple stick.

BEACH BUM

Just the thing for those blazing days on the sand.

USE 10-ounce Collins glass

For each serving, combine in pitcher or cocktail shaker:
3 ounces pineapple juice
3 ounces orange juice

Stir or shake until well mixed. Pour over ice and garnish with pineapple stick.

SURFER

The most popular face on the beach, with a touch of foam.

USE 10-ounce Collins glass

For each serving, combine in pitcher:
3 ounces pineapple juice
3 ounces orange juice
2 ounces ginger ale

Stir and pour over ice. Top with slightly sweetened, stiffly beaten egg white. Serve with straw.

ORANGE TINGLE

Juice and spice and sparkle equal fun.

USE 10-ounce Highball glass

For each serving, combine in pitcher:

3 ounces orange juice
1 ounce cranberry juice
½ teaspoon Rose's Lime Juice

Stir well to mix. Pour over 3 ice cubes and garnish with lime slice.

CUCUMBER POLYNESIAN

A pleasing fruit-vegetable blend.

USE 8-ounce tumbler

For each serving, combine in blender:

¼ average cucumber, peeled
6 ounces pineapple juice

Blend until smooth (about 20 seconds).
Serve over 2 ice cubes. Float cucumber slice in glass.

MELON MADNESS

Crazy about the summery taste of melon? Try it this way.

USE 10-ounce goblets or small hollowed melon shells.

For two servings, combine in blender:
1½ to 2 cups cantaloupe, honeydew or other melon
6 ounces pineapple juice
2 ounces honey

Blend 45 seconds. Pour and serve garnished with lime slice.

BLENDER
WATERMELON

Simple and delicious; pre-sweetened by Mother Nature.

USE 8-ounce glass

For each serving, combine in blender:
10 ounces watermelon, cut and seeds removed

Blend 20 seconds or sufficient time to liquefy. Strain if desired, pour over ice and serve.

MEDITERRANEAN HOLIDAY

The glory that was Greece, the grandeur that was Rome, and a frothy crown that reminds you of spindrift.

USE 10-ounce highball glass

For each serving, combine in blender:

1 cup strawberries
6 ounces white grape juice
1 ounce confectioner's sugar

Blend 30 seconds and pour into glass. Top with:

½ egg white, beaten with ½ ounce superfine sugar to form peaks.

Serve with straw.

FLORIDA KISS

Call it a California Kiss if you like; the versatile taste can go anywhere.

USE 8-ounce Old-fashioned glass

For each serving, combine in pitcher:

2 ounces grapefruit juice
2 ounces orange juice
2 ounces lemon-lime soda

Stir gently, pour over ice, garnish with lemon wedge, and enjoy!

ORCHARD

A pleasing blend of favorite fruit flavors.

USE 10-ounce stemmed goblet, sugar-frosted
For each serving, combine in pitcher:
2 ounces grapefruit juice
2 ounces orange juice
2 ounces apple juice
2 ounces white grape juice

Stir gently, serve over three ice cubes, garnished with an orange slice.

SUNSET SERENADE

A sweet song in harmony.

USE 10-ounce Collins glass
For one serving, combine in glass (in order):
1 ounce grenadine syrup
Crushed ice to fill glass
3 ounces orange juice
3 ounces pineapple juice

Serve without  stirring.

RAZZMATAZZ

Another fruity-cool specialty to brighten the dog days.

USE 10-ounce Collins glass, sugar-frosted.

For each serving, combine in blender:

½ ripe banana
2 ice cubes
2 ounces juice from canned red raspberries or raspberry syrup
½ ounce lemon juice
1 ounce confectioner's sugar (½ ounce if raspberry syrup is used)
3 ounces lemon-lime soda

Blend 30-40 seconds or until slushy. Pour and serve.

KIWI FIZZ

Starring that ugly-delicious little Down Under delicacy.

USE 8-ounce tumbler or water goblet

For each serving, combine in blender:

1 Kiwi fruit, peeled and cut in pieces
1 ounce simple syrup
1 drop green vegetable coloring
1 dash mint cooking extract

Blend until fruit is liquified. Pour in glass and add:

4 ounces club soda
3 ice cubes

Stir and serve.

LUNA

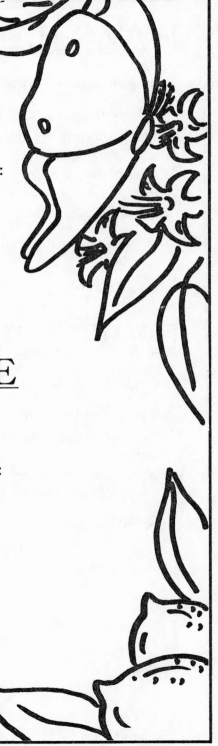

The cool, ethereal color of those fairylike creatures you sometimes see on a summer night.

USE 10-ounce Collins glass

For each serving, combine in glass:
1 teaspoon Rose's Lime Juice
6 ounces lemon-lime soda
2 scoops lime sherbet

Serve with straw and long spoon. Garnish with lime slice.

ROLLS ROYCE

Smooth and sophisticated.

USE 10-ounce Collins glass

For each serving, combine in glass:
1 teaspoon lemon juice
½ ounce simple syrup
6 ounces lemon-lime soda
2 scoops lemon sherbet

Garnish with lemon slice.
Serve with straw and long spoon.

HAWAIIAN SUNSET

An elegant sherbet drink for dessert or a hot afternoon.

USE 10-ounce Collins glass
For each serving, combine in glass:
1 teaspoon grenadine
2 ounces pineapple juice
6 ounces lemon-lime soda
1 scoop pineapple sherbet

Serve with straw and long spoon.

PEACH PUNCH

Just right for a small celebration.

USE punch cups or small winestems
For four servings, combine in blender:
2 peaches
1 average slice cantaloupe
1 scoop pineapple sherbet

Blend 30 seconds, pour and serve.

BANANA SUNTAN

Add a spark to two delicious flavors for a bright surprise.

USE 8-ounce Old-fashioned glass
For each serving, combine in blender:
½ banana
¾ ounce creme de cocoa sauce
1 scoop vanilla ice cream
1 dash mint cooking extract
2 ice cubes

Blend 45 seconds, serve garnished with mint sprig.

BANANA-CHOCOLATE SHAKE

Two heavenly flavors blended icy-cold.

USE 10-ounce highball glass
For each serving, combine in blender:
1 banana
1 large scoop vanilla ice cream
½ ounce chocolate syrup
3 ounces milk
3 ounces club soda

Blend 30 seconds.

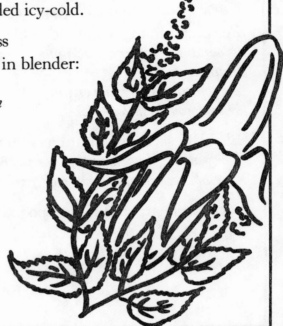

GEORGIA MOONLIGHT

Smooth and sweet as a honeysuckle-scented Southern summer night.

USE 10-ounce Collins glass
For each serving, combine in blender:
1 fresh peach
1 scoop vanilla ice cream
4 ounces Wink

Blend until smooth. Pour and serve garnished with fresh peach slice.

PINKIE

Something more than a strawberry milk shake.

USE 11-ounce highball glass
For each serving, combine in blender:
½ ounce strawberry colada mix
6 ounces milk
2 scoops strawberry ice cream
½ teaspoon fresh lime juice

Blend 15 seconds or until just mixed. Top with:
½ egg white, beaten with 1 teaspoon sugar and 1 drop red vegetable coloring, to form stiff peaks.

Serve with straw and long spoon. Garnish with strawberry.

BLACKBERRY SHAKE

A luscious summertime treat.

USE 10-ounce Collins glass

For each serving, combine in saucepan:
8 ounces fresh blackberries
3 ounces simple syrup
Heat, and strain to extract syrup.
Combine in blender:
4 ounces blackberry syrup
4 ounces milk
2 scoops vanilla ice cream

Blend 15 seconds, pour and serve.

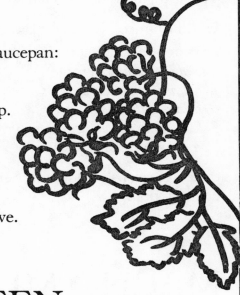

SILVER QUEEN

Royal and unique.

USE 10-ounce highball glass

For each serving, combine in glass:
2 scoops vanilla ice cream
4 ounces white grape juice
2 ounces club soda

Stir gently. Serve with straw
and long spoon.

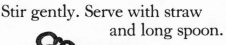

WEST INDIES

Tropical glamour, with a slightly naughty aura.

USE 11-ounce Highball glass

For each serving, combine in cocktail shaker:

2 scoops vanilla ice cream
1½ ounces cream of coconut
6 ounces milk
1 dash rum-flavored cooking extract
4 ounces club soda

Shake vigorously and pour. Serve with sweetened whipped cream topping.

MACHO MUSCLE

So nutritious, it probably could substitute for lunch.

USE 11-ounce tumbler

For each serving, combine in blender:

1 egg
1 ounce vanilla-flavored powdered protein
1 ounce creamy peanut butter
1 ounce honey
½ banana
6 ounces orange juice

Blend 1 minute or until smooth. Pour and serve.

FRAMBOISETTE

Sweet and fruity, a perfect summer stand-in for dessert.

USE 11-ounce Collins glass or two 5½-ounce cocktail glasses.

For one large or two small servings, combine in blender:
6 ounces lemon-lime soda
2 scoops raspberry sherbet
3 ounces canned red raspberries and juice
2 ounces light cream

Blend 15 seconds at low speed. Pour and serve.
Garnish with raspberries or lime slice.

BANDANNA

Tropical tastes born for each other.

USE 6-ounce cocktail glass

For each serving, combine in blender:
1 banana
1 ounce cream of coconut
1 ounce light cream
3 ice cubes

Blend 45 seconds, pour and serve.

PINEAPPLE-BERRY FREEZE

Sweet and cool, to quench a midsummer dry spell.

USE 10-ounce Collins glass

For each serving, combine in blender:
1 cup strawberries, hulled and cut in pieces
½ ounce simple syrup
Blend 15 seconds. Add:
2 scoops pineapple sherbet
2 ounces pineapple juice
4 ounces lemon-lime soda

Blend 10 more seconds. Serve with straw.

MINTLOPE

Sun-ripened melon, ice cream and a hint of mint give this adaptable charmer an exciting personality. Use your own favorite flavor of ice cream.

USE 10-ounce Collins glass

For two servings, combine in blender:
2 cups cantaloupe
¼ teaspoon mint cooking extract
Blend to liquefy cantaloupe. Add:
2 scoops ice cream

Blend 10 more seconds, pour and serve.

ICED MINT COFFEE

If you like iced coffee, you'll love it like this.

USE 10-ounce Collins glass

For each serving, combine in glass:
3 ice cubes
6 ounces strong hot coffee
2 teaspoons superfine sugar
Stir to melt ice. Add:
2 teaspoons creme de menthe syrup
½ teaspoon mint cooking extract
1 scoop vanilla ice cream

Stir again and serve.

HOT MINT CHOCOLATE

A time-tested way to make a good thing better.

USE 6-ounce cocoa mug

For each serving, combine in mug:
5-6 ounces HOT CHOCOLATE (see recipe)
¼ teaspoon mint cooking extract

Stir and serve. Garnish with marshmallows or mint.

COCOA MEDITERRANEAN

The best of two worlds.

USE standard cocoa mug

For each serving, combine in mug:
5-6 ounces HOT CHOCOLATE (see recipe)
1 teaspoon grenadine
Juice of 1/8 orange

Drop squeezed shell of orange in mug.
Serve immediately.

MOKO COCOA

For mocha-lovers with emphasis
on the chocolate.

USE standard teacup and mug

For each serving, combine in
cup or mug:
5-6 ounces HOT CHOCOLATE
(see recipe)
1/2 teaspoon instant coffee

Stir and serve.

Chapter Seven

◆

Most
Valuable
Punches

Chapter Seven
◆

Unquestionably, these are the star players in the biggest "bowl game" of all. Whatever the celebration, the punch bowl's presence creates an air of conviviality, a gathering place as well as a source of refreshment. Topped with colorful floating slices of fruit or creamy foam, made from a secret recipe or a commercial mix, punch on the party table creates a spirit of festivity and abundance. Enjoy these delightful recipes anytime you want to make a gathering really special.

CHAMPAGNE-STYLE PUNCH

Perfect for weddings and other gala celebrations. If the guests don't notice "the difference," don't tell them!

For each 5 cups, combine in separate container:

8 ounces orange juice
2 ounces lime juice
4 ounces superfine sugar

Stir until sugar is dissolved, and chill thoroughly.
Combine in chilled punch bowl with:

1 liter sparkling white grape juice or
de-alcoholized sparkling white wine.

Stir gently and serve.

FLORIDA PUNCH

Sings with citrus flavor and a spicy sparkle.

Combine in saucepan:

16 ounces superfine sugar
24 ounces water
Stir over low heat to dissolve sugar. Cool. Add to:
1½ quarts orange juice
1½ quarts grapefruit juice
12 ounces lime juice
Pour over ice mold or ice cubes in punch bowl. Add:
1½ quarts ginger ale

Stir and serve. Garnish with citrus fruit slices.

TEA PUNCH

A familiar guest at parties since at least the 19th century; maybe longer.

Combine in punch bowl:

Ice mold or large piece of ice
1 pint strong tea
1 pint club soda or ginger ale
1½ quarts fruit juice

Sweeten with simple syrup to taste, depending on kind of fruit juice used.

SUMMER HARVEST PUNCH

An exquisite blend of fruit and ice cream.

Combine in blender:

12 ounces watermelon, cut in pieces
4 peaches, peeled and cut small
1 cup fresh strawberries
8 ounces apple juice
1 pint vanilla ice cream

Blend at high speed about 20 seconds or until smooth.
Makes about 1 quart.

SHERBET PUNCH

Freeze ice in a fancy gelatine mold for an easy touch of
glamour.

Combine in punch bowl:

Large piece of ice or several ice cubes
1 pint orange sherbet
1 quart ginger ale

Stir and garnish with mint sprigs.

SOUTHERN CALIFORNIA PUNCH

Another delicious citrus punch, with a western accent.

Combine in punch bowl:
Ice mold or several ice cubes
8 ounces simple syrup
24 ounces lemon juice
1 quart orange juice
8 ounces pineapple juice
2 quarts ginger ale, chilled

Stir and garnish with citrus slices or mint leaves.

JULY JUBILEE PUNCH

Combine in blender:
3 pears, peeled and cut small
3 peaches, peeled and cut small
3 bananas, sliced
Blend until smooth. Add to:
3 ounces Passionfruit syrup
6 scoops strawberry ice cream
12 ounces lemon-lime soda
3 ounces grape juice

Stir to blend; serve immediately.

PINEAPPLE ICE CREAM PUNCH

Creamy, sweet and smooth. For very special occasions.

Combine in punch bowl:

1 pint vanilla ice cream
1 pint pineapple sherbet
1 quart pineapple juice, chilled
1 quart ginger ale, chilled

Stir to break up ice cream and sherbet. Serve.

EGG NOG

Christmas spirit without spirits. Of course, the other kind is more frequently served, but a surprising number of people enjoy it "plain." If your house is on their visiting intinerary, your guests will thank you for keeping their trip a safe one.

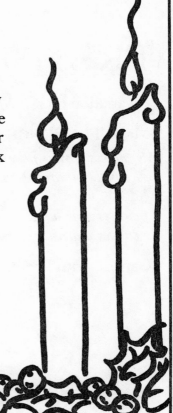

Combine in punch bowl:

4 eggs, beaten with:
2 ounces superfine sugar
½ teaspoon salt. Add:
1 teaspoon vanilla cooking extract
1 quart milk

Stir to mix. Top with grated nutmeg.

SPICY LEMONADE

Another twist for an old-fashioned standby.

Combine in saucepan:
8 ounces simple syrup
½ ounce whole cloves
1 stick cinnamon
Simmer 5 minutes. Combine with:
Juice and shells of 3 lemons
Let stand 2 hours, strain into:
1 quart water

Serve over ice mold or ice cubes.

FRUIT FIESTA PUNCH

A variation on an old-fashioned friend.

Make TEA PUNCH (see recipe) using:
24 ounces orange juice
24 ounces pineapple juice
Add:
4 ounces lime juice
4 ounces maraschino syrup

Garnish with lemon slices.

Chapter Eight

·———◆———·

What Goes
with
What

Chapter Eight

◆

Of course, there's almost always a reason for a party: a holiday, special achievement, birthday, anniversary, going away, or coming home. Between the reasons, it's easy to find an excuse: nostalgia, fund-raising, good weather, bad weather, or just "getting together." There are mocktails for every party occasion, and their bright, fresh flavor enhaces the taste of good food. Whether your paties are alcohol-free, or whether you offer refreshments "with and without," the following suggestions will give you a "feel" for the right combinations. The suggested menus are traditional, rather than boldy innovative. You get to supply the originality. Add, subtract and change as you see fit, but here are the ideas to start with, for every season.

SPRING FLINGS

BUSINESS TEAS Pleasant spring weather provides businessmen and women with the incentive to get outside the office to discuss their transactions. Whether at an elegant hotel or a conference room, the "power tea" menu is quite simple:

> Finger sandwiches
> Cookies or small tarts
> Hot tea

MEMBERSHIP PARTIES Fraternal, social and service organizations often hold membership drives and entertain prospective members in spring. Much will depend on the size, nature and tradition of the group, but with the possible exception of street gangs, most clubs have some members who prefer a non-alcoholic drink.

If your membership parties usually feature a bar, keg or sherry-sipping, it's a small matter to add a bartender who knows mocktails, a crate of soda, or a pot of high-quality tea, without spoiling the atmosphere.

If your organization is holding its first such get-together, it will probably be in a home or meeting room, with donated refreshments. Keep it friendly and simple, so the organizers will have plenty of time to greet and get to know the prospects.

The following list provides some ideas to choose from, in preparing your menu:

> Finger sandwiches (Chicken salad, ham salad, and pimiento cheese are good staples.)
>
> Ham biscuits (These miniature sandwiches are almost a requirement in Virginia and some other Southern areas. Your state may have its own specialty.)
>
> Peeled shrimp with cocktail sauce
>
> Fruit and vegetable trays with dip
>
> Nuts
>
> Cookies and other sweets as provided by members from favorite recipes
>
> Sheet cake, decorated with club emblem or logo
>
> Mints
>
> Coffee
>
> Tea
>
> Sherbet Punch (Easy to make, easy to replenish and leftover ingredients can be saved for later use.)

Crudités combine well with a bleu cheese dip, or select your own favorite. An easy dip for fruit segments can be made by combining cream cheese, sugar, vanilla extract and milk to desired texture and taste.

SPRING LUNCHEONS Light food and cheerful conversations celebrate a rejuvenative season. Plan your menu around cold sliced meat or a favorite poultry or egg dish, and complement the gentle flavors with fruity, sparkling beverages designed to be noticed.

Menu #1

Sliced baked chicken

Sliced baked ham

Raisin-carrot or congealed vegetable salad

Parsley potatoes or candied sweet potatoes

Cloverleaf rolls

*Fruit juice combination drink, preferably with ginger ale
or lemon-lime soda for sparkle. Examples are Pilgrim Father,
Pilgrim Mother, Ginger-Ice Cooler, Golden Wedding
and Locomotive.*

Menu #2

Chicken or turkey casserole, or quiche

Cole slaw (your favorite recipe) or shredded lettuce

Popovers

BASEBALL BUFFET   Celebrate the season opener with a sandwich bar after the game, or during it if the gang comes over to watch after TV.

Sliced cold meats (chicken, ham and roast beef, or pre-pared cold cuts)

Assorted sliced cheeses

Assortment of sliced bread and sandwich rolls

Mustard, mayonnaise, horseradish, catsup

Lettuce, radishes, olives, pickles, sliced tomatoes

Coleslaw

Potato salad

Macaroni salad

Cucumber and onion slices in vinegar or sour cream

Chips, dips and nuts

Fruit bowl

Coffee

Soft drinks — variety of flavors

WEDDING AND BABY SHOWERS The basic purpose is to give gifts to the bride-to-be or expected baby. Guests are close friends, and rarely does the menu become elaborate. Refreshments can consist of a dessert with coffee or tea, or can include:

> Crackers and melba toast with dips and spreads
> Chicken salad puffs
> Crudités with dip
> Sheet cake
> Decorated cupcakes or petit fours
> Nuts
> Mints
> Peach Punch

ST. PATRICK'S DAY PARTIES You don't have to be Irish to celebrate a break from the somber temperatures and clouds of March. if you have a lot of authentic "auld sod" recipes, you'll probably want to show them off. Otherwise, you can create the spirit with:

> Corned beef and cabbage
> Boiled potatoes
> Scones
> Hot tea

If it isn't a dinner party, you may serve shortbread cookies and Mint Lemonade, or just invite friends over for Katydids.

EASTER BREAKFAST After the Sunrise Service, it's nice to have Grandma and Grandpa over for a special breakfast. It's especially nice if you're going over to the *other* grandparents' house for a holiday dinner. Make it festive with flowers on the table, and:

> Colored hard-boiled eggs, or
> Scrambled eggs in toast baskets
> Fruit cup or ambrosia
> Fried ham or Canadian bacon
> Apple-cinnamon or blueberry muffins

> 4-ounce servings of Virgin Mary, Royal Purple, Beach
>   Bum, Alligator, and bottled cranberry-raspberry
> Café l'Orange
> Cocoa Mediterranean or Parisette for the children

Apple-cinnamon muffins can be made by adding to a commercial muffin mix: one chopped apple, and crumbled mixture of butter, brown sugar and cinnamon.

DINNER PARTIES French and Oriental dinners are especially appropriate for spring dinner parties. Because you will probably have your own preferred delicacies, no menu is provided. However, some suggestions can be made about the beverages to serve.

For the mocktail hour before dinner, serve the Taiwan, Gimmeit, Horse's Neck or Orange Tingle with the Oriental meal, and tea at the table. Americans are accustomed to drinking tea with Chinese and Japanese food, and it always goes well. With the French dinner, a Noel Coward, Diabolo Menthe, Fuschia or Glacier may be the mocktail, and a faux wine will go nicely with dinner.

BIRTHDAY PARTIES   For children's parties, Juicy Punch or cola. For adults, a mocktail bar with a variety of possibilities, or something glamorous like Razzmatazz, Silver Queen or Blue Lagoon. Fresh strawberry drinks, such as Jasmine, are especially nice for small parties.

GLADD PROM PARTIES   All over America, those wonderful people in MADD and SADD are organizing all-night bashes on Prom Night and Graduation Night. Just to put a more positive title on the celebration, (meaning no disparagement to those fine organizations) we'll call it GLADD (Good Leadership Avoids Driving Disasters.) Whether the all-night activity is skating, swimming, a concert, or more dancing, you'll need two menus: one for immediately after the prom, and another for breakfast.

HORS D'OEUVRES MENU   In addition to all the "expected" snacks such as chips, mini-pizzas, finger sandwiches, include some of the less ordinary, "adult" munchies such as:

> Avocado slices on vegetable tray
>   (also raw sweet potato slices)
> Smoked oysters or clams
> Artichoke hearts
> Chicken livers in bacon
> Liver paté
> Ripe olives
> Caviar

If the prom has featured a faux champagne fountain or bottles of sparkling grape juice on the tables, have a full mocktail bar, with lots of fruit and soda possibilities. If the mocktail bar was set up at the prom, have the faux champagne now.

BREAKFAST BUFFET   Scrambled eggs
> Waffles
> Biscuits
> Creamed chipped beef
> Toast
> Large assortment of fresh fruits and berries
> Corned beef hash
> Fried potatoes
> Grits (in places where grits are recognized)
> Individually boxed cereals
> Variety of juices
> Coffee, tea, hot chocolate, milk

MEMORIAL DAY PARTIES   The first "cookout occasion" of the year has a bad reputation for drunk-driving accidents. It's a great time to introduce your friends to your mocktail-making prowess, and a perfect time to enjoy a backyard celebration, without going far from home. Let the neighbors contribute some of the menu, if you like:

Mocktails before dinner: Surfer, Crocodile, Cola Libre, Kamehameha, etc.

Steaks, hamburgers or frankfurters

Baked beans and specialty casseroles

Carrot and celery sticks, spring onions

Lettuce and sliced tomato

Salads, deviled eggs

Hot dog and hamburger rolls

Mustard, mayonnaise, catsup, relish, etc.

Potato chips

Dessert drinks with ice cream or sherbet: Framboisette, Hawaiian Sunset, Georgia Moonlight, Chocolate soda.

SUMMER CELEBRATIONS

GLADD GRADUATION PARTY   The Graduation Party will be similar to the Prom Party, with the probable exception that it will be more informal, and may include a buffet supper. A chicken barbeque or other picnic-type supper should be appropriate, but again, lesser-known foods, for example, such tropical fruits as kiwi, mango and papaya, can be made available. This way, the substance associated with a special Rite of Passage can be something harmless.

SUMMER LUNCHEONS   When vacationing relatives and old friends come to visit, an easy way to entertain is with a light lunch. It doesn't have to be a lot of work, and if you like, the beverage can double as dessert. All you need are:

Sandwiches (Club, BLT, tuna salad, egg, crab or chicken salad)

Salad (Potato, macaroni, or congealed vegetable salad in individual molds)

Limeade, milk shakes, or ice cream sodas.

THEATRE PARTIES　After those outdoor plays, operas, and concerts, when it's just "too nice a night" to stop having fun, invite everyone over for a frosty drink on the lawn and some good conversation. Some possibilities include:

> Strawberry or Banana Mocquiri
> Piña Con Nada
> Iced Mint Coffee
> Lemon Soda
> Luna
> Rolls-Royce

PICNICS, BARBEQUES, BRUNSWICK STEWS, SEAFOOD FESTS　From sea to shining sea, your area has its own traditional "outdoor" meal, the kind that goes with political campaigns, fund-raisers, and family reunions. Besides canned or bottled soft drinks, some easy beverages for these festivities are:

> Lemonade
> Iced tea
> Coffee

TENNIS AND SWIMMING PARTIES　To cool down an active body, and replenish its energy supply, active summer sports can stop for a few minutes for a welcome break of:

> Annie Sunshine
> East and West
> Beach Bum

LAWN PARTIES　A lovely old-fashioned custom, and a pleasant diversion for a young teen-ager who'd like to try her hand at being a hostess. Let her do the baking.

> Chocolate chip or sugar cookies, or brownies
> Pink Lemonade

ITALIAN DINNERS   Sunny summer must be reminiscent of sunny Italy, because Italian dinners are especially popular during the season. Show off your "pasta power" with a meal like this:

> Antipasto-relish tray
> Your choice of main dish: cannelone, tetrazinni,
>   spaghetti, etc.
> Broccoli, zucchini or eggplant
> Bread sticks or garlic bread
> Faux Bordeaux or Faux Sparkling Burgundy

LUAUS   For a real luau, there *has* to be a roast pig, so it's going to be a big party or there's going to be more leftover pork than you can imagine. You'll probably have this party catered, so when it comes to the beverage, arrange for a fruit punch such as our Juicy Punch, or include a juice bar, with plenty of tropical goodies like the Piña Con Nada, Kamehameha, Blue Lagoon, and Wahine.

WEDDINGS   Wedding receptions are also usually big enough to be catered, but for a small buffet reception, you can be equally elegant with smaller version of the membership Party menu, accompanied by Summer Harvest Punch or Pineapple Ice Cream Punch.

INDEPENDENCE DAY PICNICS   For fun, have a covered-dish picnic with a "Gay Nineties" theme. Let each guest dig up a turn-of-the-century recipe, and serve fried chicken, home-made pie and ice cream. Put on a Sousa record, dress in costume if you like, and feature these drinks:

> Pink Lemonade
> Black Cow
> Shrinking Violet
> Raspberry Vinegar
> Chocolate, lemon and strawberry soda

FALL FESTIVITIES

LABOR DAY PARTIES   This will probably be your last big cookout before putting away the grill for the winter. You've been practicing all summer; now bring out the good stuff!

> Steaks, barbecued ribs or shish kebabs
> Salads, casseroles, roast corn and potatoes
> Plenty of desserts
> Princess Di, Lemonade, assorted soft drinks and coffee.

FOOTBALL PARTIES   Tailgate Parties have become a great way of spending the time that passes while the parking lot clears. They may be elaborate, incuding steaks from a portable grill, or simple, with sandwiches and perhaps a casserole or salad. One thing they all have in common is guests who are about to drive home in heavy traffic. Bottled or canned soft drinks are easily carried around in warmer weather, and a jug of coffee or hot chocolate will be a welcome respite from colder weather. For smaller parties, a container of hot water with instant coffee, tea bags, and cocoa packages will save space.

If the celebration is at home, the weather will still affect the menu. In early fall, a "football hero" buffet can pick up some of its ideas from the baseball buffet, but feature spicy deli meats and cheeses, and hero or hoagie sandwich rolls. Complement these with:

> Clam Juice Cocktail
> Beefy Bracer
> Virgin Marie
> Horse's Neck
> Motorcycle

Later in the season, change to warmer dishes, such as:

> Hot chicken nuggets or wing dings
> Scalloped oysters or oyster stew

Sweet Potato or pumpkin pudding
Corn Pudding
Hamburger pie
Potatoes au gratin
Green bean or broccoli casserole
Assortment of Salads
Cheese Fondu
Moko Cocoa
Hot Grapefruit Toddy
Coffee Mediterranean
Cola
Ginger Ale, lemon-lime soda

WINE AND CHEESE PARTIES   If you're having a traditional wine and cheese party, you may wish merely to add some bottled sparkling grape juice and sparkling unfermented cider to the array of wines. If you're breaking ground with an alcohol-free party, serve each faux wine in a pretty carafe and provide:

Variety of cheeses
Crisp crackers
Fruit Tray

FIFTIES NOSTALGIA   These parties are currenty popular, not only among those who have fun dragging out those old clothes left over from high school, but among the teen-agers who enjoy showing Mom and Dad how silly they used to look. Get out the Elvis records, poodle skirts and ducktails, dance the bop and enjoy:

Pizza
Cheeseburgers
French fries and onion rings
Small candy bars: Baby Ruth nuggets, Butterfinger
    chips and Hershey miniatures, peanut blocks and
    peppermint patties

Brownies
Chips
Limeade
Chocolate sodas and milk shakes
Rum and Coke; Hold the Rum
Black and Tan

FALL LUNCHEONS   Midday meetings abound in Autumn,
as schools and organizations prepare for a hard winter's work.
Even lighter meals are more substantial than those served in
the warmer seasons. Here are two possibilities for a nourishing
lift that will help you face the afternoon's business:

Menu #1

Cheese souffle

Waldorf Salad

Biscuits with butter

Faux Chablis or Club Cocktail

Coffee or tea

Menu #2

Beef Pot Pie

Cole slaw with green peppers and radishes

Wheat rolls

Faux Port or Noel Coward

Coffee or tea

LEAF-RAKING PARTIES   An opportunity to enjoy the glor-
ious outdoor magic of Indian summer, and to make fun out of
work. Brush off the picnic table one more time, and reward the
rakers with:

Chocolate chip cookies
Hot Mint Chocolate

HALLOWE'EN PARTIES   Many communities are holding parties for youngsters, to protect them from the dangers of trick-or-treating. If your neighborhood has such a project, you may want to include:

> Doughnut holes
> Brownies
> Apples
> Candy and popcorn balls
> Hot Chocolate

If you include guests from the senior citizens' home, add:

> Hot Spiced Cider

If it's a teen-age party, add chips and Party Mix.

NEAR EASTERN DINNER   The crisp Autumn air encourages just the sort of appetite for spicy-rich Arabic, Indian or Israeli dishes. Faux wines go well with these, or try the traditional Abdug or Lassi.

THANKSGIVING DINNER   The Thanksgiving feast is always big enough to make sure everyone knows what to be thankful about. An old Colonial menu called for turkey, chicken, chicken pie, potatoes, squash, onions, gravy, apple and cranberry sauce, oyster sauce, two kinds of bread, two puddings, and three kinds of pie.

While the most popular items haven' t changed much, every family has its own special meal, and its own preference of beverages. For something new, try Tea Punch with apple and cranberry juices, or Pilgrim Mother.

MOCKTAIL PARTIES   When indoor entertaining begins, you're able to show off your health awareness, and cater to that of others. A number of "natural" party snacks, such as nuts, banana chips, and health-food mixes can be found at the supermarket or at the vitamin store. Stock up your mocktail bar for several standards and a few spectaculars, and you're on your way.

> Health-food Party mix, nuts, etc.
> Crudités with dip
> Fruit with cheese
> Mocktail bar

FUN FOR THE FREEZIN' SEASON

APRÉS SKI OR ICE-SKATING PARTIES   Very simple, very glamorous. Pick up a variety of doughnuts from your local doughnut shop, serve warm if possible, or bring your own home-made kind fresh from the kitchen. Accompany with one or more of:

> Hot Spiced Cider
> Hot Chocolate (one of the flavored kinds, if you like)
> Hot Grapefruit Toddy

BASKETBALL, BOWLING OR ROLLER-SKATING BUFFET   Model your sandwich bar after those prepared for baseball and football seasons. Neither spectators nor participants in indoor sports will need as much warming-up as football fans, so the mocktails or punch won't need to be supplemented by hot drinks unless it's a *very* cold day, but keep a pot of coffee on hand.

NINETEENTH CENTURY PARTIES   Perhaps it's because of Dickens and Clement Clarke Moore, but we tend to connect the words "Victorian" and "Christmas." With the increasing popularity of 19th century dance workshops and Civil War Reenactment groups, many of us have 1800's costumes around, and the "historical evening" becomes more and more popular. Dances of the period were lavish, all-night affairs with sumptuous dinners, so the degree of authenticity may depend on budget and other practical considerations. A carefully researched meal or a covered-dish buffet with "old family recipes" is appropriately teamed with coffee or tea. As refreshments during your dance, you'll want fruit cake, of course, and dainty old-fashioned cookies. Combine with:

> Tea Punch
> Egg Nog

PIZZA PARTIES   Only two items, a fun warm-up lunch on a snowy day, after sledding, shoveling walks, or just plain playing.

> Pizza
> Cola

CHRISTMAS BRUNCH   A popular way of being neighborly, this late-morning breakfast-lunch combination is typically American. So is this international combination of delicacies.

> Mona Lisa, Clam Juice Cocktail, Oramato, or
>   Cucumber Polynesian
> Bacon or ham quiche
> Waffles
> Sweetened cooked apples, cherries or pineapple
> Hash brown potatoes
> Link sausage
> Sliced bananas with milk or cream
> Hot mince pie
> Stollen and Scandinavian holiday bread
> Russian Tea

CHRISTMAS DINNER Like Thanksgiving dinner, only more so, this particular feast is so steeped in tradition that only the bravest and most beloved family cook had better initatie a change. Carbonated beverages will be easier on the digestive system of the 14-year-old who proves he's an adult by eating everything in sight, and keep the egg nog around for all the drop-in visitors; serve it with those elegant Christmas cookies and fruit cake. For those who don't drink egg nog, cola drinks usually fill the bill. Merry Christmas!

WINTER LUNCHEONS For good friends who aren't immediate family, it's acceptable to serve Christmas Dinner Leftovers, at a holiday-season dinner. But they mustn't *look* like leftovers. Here are a few ideas:

> Turkey-vegetable soup, congealed salad, homemade bread
> East and West
> Mince or Pumpkin Pie
> French Onion soup, Venison or roast beef on Kaiser roll, tomato aspic
> Angostura Cocktail
> Fruitcake and egg nog
> Pork with barbecue sauce on roll, coleslaw, applesauce
> Princess Di
> Ice cream and holiday cookies
> Chicken or turkey salad sandwich, fried sliced potatoes
> Horse's Neck or Safedriver
> Gelatin with whipped cream
> Ham-rice casserole, grean beans amandine, crescent rolls
> Hawaiian Orange Juice
> Plum Pudding

NEW YEAR'S EVE PARTIES   Most private parties on New Year's Eve are not the all-night kind, but begin after dinner and end before dawn. Larger than the Mocktail Party, they can feature:

> Broiled chicken livers
> Batter-fried mushrooms and other vegetables
> Swedish meatballs
> Melba toast with warm crab or chicken dip
> Cheese fondue
> Ham biscuits
> Vegetable and fruit trays
> Faux Champagne and Faux Pink Champagne

MEXICAN DINNER PARTY   The bright colors of Mexican decoration and bright, spicy taste of Mexican food make a perfect antidote to the dreary, bleak feel of those long winter months. Set off your chimichangas and tacos with:

> Cola Libre
> Mosquito
> Miami

VALENTINE'S DAY PARTIES   Cozy mini-parties for two, to sit by the fire and pretend it's spring, while you make plans for June — and forever.

> Puerto Rican Pink Lady
> Pinkie

AFTER-DINNER DRINKS   For one of those special "little drinks" that's served in place of dessert, try:

> Prism
> Prince Alphonse
> Katydid
> Russian Defector

Index